THE HERO

A comparison of

CHIEF CRAZY HORSE

and

FIELD MARSHAL

ROMMEL

Published by
Wicóni Wasté
P.O. Box 480005
Denver, CO 80248
Copyright © 2002
by Allen Ross-Ehanamani

First Printing, March 2003

LIBRARY OF CONGRESS CATALOGING
IN PUBLICATION DATA.

Ross-Ehanamani, Allen
The Hero, a comparison of
Chief Crazy Horse & Field Marshal Rommel,

Bibliography: Crazy Horse p.72 Rommel P.157

ISBN 0-9726414-0-8

ACKNOWLEDGMENTS

All people of the Oceti Sakowin

All Sun Dancers

My Wife:	Dorothy Brave Eagle for her patience, understanding and love.
My Typist:	Karen Rayman / Lonee' Roy
My Astrologer:	Mary Jayn / Kim Marie
Artist:	Marty Red Bear
My Printer:	Charles Hohnstein

My children and grandchildren

A special thanks to my spirit guides for making this book possible.

TABLE OF CONTENTS

Section II Field Marshal Rommel

Section III

Section IV

CHIEF CRAZY HORSE

" All he wanted was to take care of his people
and preserve their way of life"

PREFACE

In 1992 my book Mitakuye Oyasin "We are all related", won a top book award at the Frankfurt Book Fair in Germany. At that time I was the superintendent of Education on the Standing Rock Reservation, located in both North Dakota and South Dakota. Standing Rock Reservation is the home of the Hunkpapa people. It was here that I met many of the descendants of the warriors who had taken part in the Battle on the Little Big Horn River. I learned from my friend, Doug White Bull, that his Great Grandfather is the White Bull I wrote about in this book. While at Standing Rock, my wife Dorothy Brave Eagle and I self published the book Mitakuye Oyasin, so we had to do all of our own marketing and sales, etc. We soon learned that we could not sell the book as long as we were employed by the Bureau of Indian Affairs. The Bureau's Personnel Department informed us of an old obsolete law that was established back when the Indian Agents and reservation Superintendents were corrupt. At that time, the agents were usually political appointees who tried to take advantage of the local Indian populations. To counteract this practice, a law was established that BIA employees and their families were forbidden to carry on any trade or business dealings with Indians. It was called "Trading with the Indians Clause". Well, this law was still on the books, so I had to resign my position with the BIA in order to market my book. In the marketing effort to sell the book I was placed in the position to go to Crazy Horse Mountain. As a result of my book signings there, I was inspired to study about the man Crazy Horse in order to answer the tourist's questions more accurately. This interest along with the fact that I knew descendants of the people I studied made my research all the more exciting. (I am a member of the Sioux Nation and was raised on the Rosebud, Pine Ridge and Flandreau Reservations in South Dakota.) I have participated in my own culture as a pow-wow contest dancer and in spiritual ceremonialism. Having participated in the Sun Dance for 25 years and being a dream interpreter, seven years ago I was put into the position of being the organizer/leader of the Black Hills Sun Dance. I am not a holy man, nor am I a medicine man, I am just an ordinary man who has studied American Indian ceremonialism for approximately 30 years. In this book, I have used information from the spirit world to answer intriguing questions about Crazy Horse and about the Battle of the Little Big Horn. To my knowledge this is the first time this technique has been used to solve these unanswered questions. Through out this book I will use the word Sioux. It is only because when I tell the tourist my traditional tribal name, they have not heard of it. But they have heard of the name Sioux. The original seven tribes are known as Oceti Sakowin (seven campfires). Today these seven tribes

are more commonly known as Sioux. (The word Sioux is a French corruption of an Ojibwa word meaning enemy). The Individual tribes are called:
- Mdewankantonwan (Spirit Water Dwellers)
- Sissetonwan (Fish Scale Dwellers)
- Wahpetonwan (Camp Among the Leaves Dwellers)
- Wahpekute (Shoots Through the Leaves Dwellers)
- Ihanktonwan (End Dwellers)
- Ihanktonwana (Little End Dwellers)
- Tetonwan (Prairie Dwellers)
The first four tribes are known collectively as the Santee. They lived primarily on the Minnesota and Mississippi Rivers in what is now the state of Minnesota. Ihanktonwan and Ihanktonwana lived in eastern and southeastern part of what is called South Dakota today. The Tetonwan tribe has seven bands called Oglala (Scatter One's Own), Sichangu (Burnt Thigh), Miniconju (Plant by Water), Itazipco (No Bows), Ohenupa (Two Kettle), Sihasapa (Black Foot), and Hunkpapa (Camp at Entrance). These seven bands lived primarily in western North Dakota, South Dakota, Nebraska, eastern Wyoming, and in southeastern Montana. The language of the seven tribes has three different dialects. The Santee group speaks Dakota, the Ihanktonwan group speaks Nakota, and the Tetonwan speak Lakota. The original nation, the Oceti Sakowin (Seven Campfires) have as one of their origin stories, that they came from an island in the Atlantic Ocean.

With this introduction I now invite the reader to sit back and enjoy an entirely different version of American Indian history.

CHAPTER 1

A BIOGRAPHY
OF CHIEF CRAZY HORSE

AN BIOGRAPHY
OF CRAZY HORSE

He was born in 1840, at the confluence of Cheyenne River and Rapid Creek.[1] He was born with light skin and brown curly hair. Hence his childhood name became Curly. Curly's father was named Crazy Horse. He belonged to the Oglala Band of the Tetonwan Tribe. He was a Holy man, a prophet and dream interpreter. Curly had an older sister named Laughing One and a younger brother named Little Hawk.

RAISED IN BLACK HILLS AREA

Curly's mother died when he was very young.[2] His mother was a Sichangu Lakota. It was her sister that took the responsibility of raising young Curly.[3] Curly's childhood friend was named Hump. Together they learned to ride and hunt. When they reached puberty they were asked to join a hunting society called the Crow Owners. The Crow Owners were also known for their protection of the people. Crazy Horse spent most of these early years on the plains east and south of the Black Hills.[4]

---

[1] *Sources say he was born around 1840-1845 either at Bear Butte or Rapid Creek.*
Author's Note: My Spirit guides have informed me he was born in 1840 at the confluence of Cheyenne River and Rapid Creek in western South Dakota. See chart on p.66
[2] *Freedman, The Life and Death of Crazy Horse, pg.9.*
[3] *Author's Note: In the Lakota culture, the mother's sister is also the mother, but the mother's brother is an uncle.*
[4] *Freedman, The Life and Death of Crazy Horse, pg. 11-12, pg.49.*

FT. LARAMIE TREATY - 1851 [5]

The Oregon Trail was established in the early 1840's. Each year immigrants using the road increased. The Sioux liked to visit these immigrants because they could receive coffee, sugar and biscuits. Traders then began to set up trading posts to trade these items to the Indians. Many traders began cheating the Indians; whiskey became a trade item, which led to more problems with the traders. In 1849 gold was discovered in California, the Holy Road became flooded with gold miners and other interested people began heading to the gold fields of California. Buffalo and other game began to flee from the Holy Road area. Favorite Sioux campsites along Platte River were destroyed because of over use. Next the white man brought cholera and small pox, which killed hundreds of Indians. Some of the warriors blamed the white man for their troubles. Raids on wagon trains and trading posts began. They increased until the white people asked the U.S. Government for protection. The result was a treaty meeting at Ft. Laramie in 1851. It was the largest gathering of plains Indians to date. Some ten thousand Indians, Sioux, Cheyenne, Crow, Shoshonis, Arapaho, Arikara, Assinaboin, Hidatsa, Mandan came to the treaty meeting. The camp was so large; horses ate all

[5] Wilson, *Wyoming Historical Tour Guide*, pg.20. *Laramie was originally two words, La Ramee, which in French means "The small branches".*

the grass, so they moved 30 miles east to Horse Creek. The government promised yearly goods and monetary payments for 50 years, in exchange the government wanted passage on the route west and to build forts along this route. [6] The Sioux were not to touch this road, hence it became the "Holy Road". [7] Also, the government would safeguard the right of the Indians against the whites. Crazy Horse was 11 years old and it was the first time he had seen a white man. The important thing to come out of the 1851 Treaty meeting was the government's misreading of tribal chiefs authority [8]

THE KILLING OF CONQUERING BEAR — 1854

Each spring many Sioux would return to Ft. Laramie to receive the goods/monetary payments promised in the 1851 Treaty. In the spring of 1854 Crazy Horse and his family were camped on the Holy Road (Oregon Trail) near Ft. Laramie. One day hundreds of people were gathering at Conquering Bear's camp. Crazy Horse who was 14 years old at that time, went to see what the excitement was all about. Upon arriving at the scene Crazy Horse asked an older man what was

[6] Freedman, The Life and Death of Crazy Horse. pg.21-23 Author's Note: The Sioux called this treaty the treaty of Horse Creek
[7] Sandoz, Crazy Horse - Strange Man of the Oglala, pg.6.
[8] McMurtry, Crazy Horse, pg.24. Author's Note: The chiefs authority extended only over their own immediate band.

TREATY OF HORSE CREEK - 1851

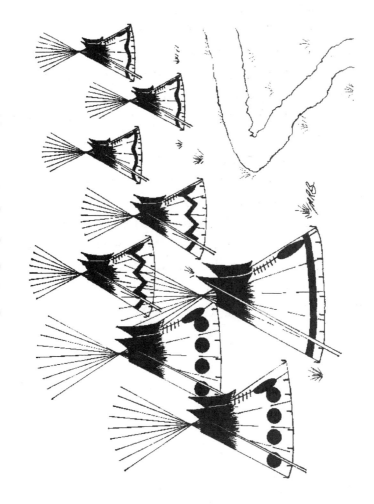

happening, the man told him that soldiers from Ft. Laramie were trying to arrest a Miniconju man for killing a lame cow. The soldiers were talking with chief Conquering Bear. But the chief told the soldiers he could not turn the man over to them because he being a Sichangu Lakota had no authority over this man. Conquering Bear then offered the man who lost the cow presents and a horse in place of the cow. The man refused saying he wanted the Miniconju arrested and put in jail. The soldiers then lined up pointed their guns at the chief and began to count. Next they began shooting. The chief fell dead. Hundreds of Sioux who were watching then attacked the soldiers and killed every one of them. [9] Later Crazy Horse learned that the soldier's leader was called Lieutenant Gratten. The soldiers killed that day numbered 32. This was the first time on the plains that soldiers were killed by Indians. [10]

[9] Freedman, The Life and Death of Crazy Horse, pg.28-30.
[10] McMurty, Crazy Horse, pg.30. * Author's Note:A french interpretor had been the cause of the Army's impulsive decision to open fire on Conquering Bear.

THE VISION OF CRAZY HORSE

After witnessing this fight Crazy Horse decided to go off by himself to ponder what he had witnessed. He was 14 years old when he went out to fast, on the third day a vision came to him. A horse with a rider emerged from a body of water and began to float in the air. The horseman was dressed in breechcloth with leggings only, and wore only one feather in his hair. His hair was unbraided, and he wore no war paint. His horse pranced and changed colors as they moved closer. A voice spoke to Crazy Horse saying, "You are to help the people with what ever need they have. You are not to take anything for yourself. If you go to war, bullets and arrows will not harm you as long as you dress in plain clothes, wear your hair unbraided with only one feather on your head and carry a small stone behind your ear. Before you mount your horse you are to throw dust over yourself and your horse." A crowd of people now appeared in the vision; they tried to hold the horseman back by grabbing onto his arms. He rode through the people and kept going. A thunderstorm appeared with hail and lightning all around, the horseman kept on riding. The storm faded, showing the horseman with hail spots on his body and a zigzag streak of lightning on his cheek. In the quiet after the storm, a red tail hawk appeared over head, his scream echoing as he flew over the horseman. Now the people appeared again grabbing at the horseman's arms, but he pulled away from them and rode off. [11] The vision ended as quickly as it started. Later Crazy Horse's father interpreted the dream for him, telling him that he was the horseman in the dream. [12]

---

[11] Freedman, *The Life and Death of Crazy Horse*, pg.31-34. *Author's Note: The dust that Crazy Horse threw over himself and his horse was from the blind mole mound. When Crazy Horse did this it would render them invisible and invulnerable to bullets and arrows.*

[12] McMurtry, *Crazy Horse*, pg.34. *Author's Note: In my experience and research on dream interpretation, I learned that any dream containing water and floating are symbolic of great spirituality. In the Lakota culture lightning plays a very symbolic role, the significance being the Thunderbeings. In my book Mitakuye Oyasin pg.130-133. I found that the Thunderbeings are the same as the Christ energy. I am not a Christian per se, but I do honor concepts found in Christianity. Also in dream interpretation, when one dreams in color it is symbolic of a great and powerful dream. In Crazy Horse's vision the horses changed color, indicating the vision was in color. For clarification, dreams and visions are synonymous, one being during sleep the other while one is awake.*

BLUE WATER MASSACRE — 1855

Crazy Horse was visiting his mother's people the summer of 1855. They were camped on the Blue Water River under the leadership of Chief Little Thunder. Little Thunder was considered a friend to the whiteman so when soldiers approached he did not expect trouble. The soldiers under General Harney were seeking revenge for the Gratten affair. They surrounded Little Thunder's camp, and accused him of taking part in the Gratten killings. Little Thunder had not been at the Gratten site; he only learned of it later, so he rightfully denied having any part of the Gratten affair. Harney did not believe him and opened fire on the Sichangu camp killing 86 men, women, and children. Crazy Horse had been away from camp chasing horses with his cousin. Upon returning to camp, the sight of so much death and destruction of innocent people filled him with hatred for the soldiers. [13]

---

[13] Freedman, *The Life and Death of Crazy Horse*, pg38-39.

GREAT GATHERING AT BEAR BUTTE — 1857

Each year the Sioux nation would come together for a visit. The meeting of friends and relatives was always a joyous occasion. The Santee's of the east would come, Ihanktonwan and Ihanktonwana of the north and the south would come and of course the Tetonwan of the west would be there. These great gatherings were first held on the James River in eastern Dakota, later the gathering was moved to the Big Bend on the Missouri River. In 1857 it was held at Bear Butte near the Black Hills.[14] The Santee's would bring guns, metal pots, knifes, and blankets for trade. These items they received from the French of the Great Lakes. The Santee traded for buffalo hides, beaver belts, porcupine quillwork and horses. Besides being a trade fair the gathering provided the chiefs an opportunity to discuss important matters such as tribal hunting areas, whiteman disease, abuse by the soldiers and of course a time to boast of their deeds. There was much dancing, Warrior society dance contests were held. The winning society would be the head warrior (Akicita) society for one year. Many social dances were also held, giving the youth time to make new friends. [15] It was at this great

---

14 *Sandoz, crazy Horse, pg. 99-100.*
15 *Ross, Mitakuye Oyasin, pg.186-192.*

gathering of 1857 that Crazy Horse met the love of his life. An Oglala girl named Black Buffalo Women. [16]

---

[16] McMurtry, Crazy Horse, pg.43.

CURLY IS GIVEN THE NAME CRAZY HORSE — 1858

Crazy Horse was now 18 years old. He was not a big man, but always ready to prove his courage. That opportunity came that summer when his people went north and west in search of game. They came upon an Arapaho camp that had many fine horses. Crazy Horse with other Oglala youths decided to raid the camp and capture their horses. Crazy Horse prepared himself the way his vision had instructed him to do. He put a small stone behind his ear, wore a single red tail hawk feather on his unbraided hair, hail spots were painted on his body and a lightning bolt painted on his face, naked except for his breechcloth and leggings. He threw dust over himself and his horse and was ready to raid the Arapaho. The Arapaho made a strong stand and the Oglala could not break it. Suddenly Crazy Horse charged forward all by himself, he rode right through the Arapaho line counting 3 coup. [17] He then turned and galloped away as arrows and bullets flew around him but none hitting him. After reaching his own men he swung his horse around and charged again. This time two Arapaho warriors rode out to meet him, he killed

17 Author's Note: Coup is a French word meaning, "to strike". In Lakota the word is yutan, meaning, "to touch the enemy". The concept was that it is more honorable to touch the enemy than to kill him.

them both and scalped them. Immediately he was shot in the leg by an Arapaho arrow. It was then that he remembered what his vision told him, "If you want protection, you must never take anything for yourself". He discarded the scalps and vowed never to take another scalp. [18]

Upon returning to his camp, Crazy Horse's father was so very proud of his son's deeds that he sponsored a feed and had a give away for him. At the giveaway Crazy Horse's father gave him his name Crazy Horse (until now Crazy Horse was called Curly). But now Curly had his adult name and his father became known by the name Worm. [19]

[18] Freedman, *The Life and Death of Crazy Horse*, pg.43-45. *Author's Note: In the 1600's on the East Coast, the Dutch offered a reward for dead Indians. A scalp was used as the method of collecting the reward. Indians originally only took scalps as a retaliatory measure.*
[19] *Ibid*, pg.46.

BROKEN HEART — 1864

The young Crazy Horse soon became a popular leader of the raids against neighboring tribes. He also became one of the best hunters of the tribe. Many times he would ride off hunting alone. Often he would stay gone for weeks. When he returned with game of buffalo, deer, elk and during seasonal migrations, geese and ducks. These he gave to the poor and elders. Crazy Horse was still living with his folks when he met Black Buffalo Women. He began to court her shortly after they met at the great gathering of Bear Butte. Black Buffalo Women was very popular and other suitors would come to call upon her as well as Crazy Horse. While gone for several weeks on one of his raids, Black Buffalo Women's parents arranged for her to marry Chief Red Cloud's nephew No Water. When Crazy Horse returned from the raid only to learn that his sweetheart had married someone else. It broke his heart. Black Buffalo Woman was forced to marry No Water because he came from an important and influential family. Crazy Horse felt so bad he went off by himself for several days. [20]

---

[20] *Ibid*, pg.48-51.

CHOSEN SHIRT WEARER — 1865

The Oglala had seven elders who were recognized as the band leaders. These elders belonged to the civil society, which had various names like; Owl Headdress, White Horse Owners, Big Belly, and Grey Eagle. [21] That year this society of elders decided to select four young men to be shirt wearers (Wokiconze Wicasa), whose duty was to put selfish interests aside and think only of the welfare of the people. As the selection began the first three were Young Man Afraid of his Horse, Sword, and American Horse. They were sons of important families. The fourth selection was Crazy Horse; it was a surprise because he was the son of a humble Holy man. [22]

---

21 Ross, *Mitakuye Oyasin*, pg.187.
22 McMurtry, *Crazy Horse*, pg.52-53. *Author's Note: A wokiconze wicasa person held a leadership position in the tribe*

HUNDRED IN THE HAND — 1866

Gold was discovered in Virginia City, Montana Territory in 1866. Soon there was a rush of whitemen trying to get there as fast as possible. The shortest route to the gold fields was straight across the Sioux reservation, even though the U.S. Government told the miners to stay out of the reservation. They crossed the reservation on a route opened by John Bozeman. The miners demanded the Army protect them as they traveled on the Bozeman Trail. General Sherman immediately started building forts along the Bozeman, while the government tried to get the Sioux to sign another treaty giving the whitemen rights to travel on and use the Bozeman Trail. [23] The treaty effort failed because the Sioux had seen how the U.S. Army was already building forts before the treaty was agreed upon. Red Cloud said to the government negotiators, "Do you think we are blind, we can see what you are doing. You treat us like children, I will talk with you no more, we will fight you for the last of our hunting grounds". Thus began the Sioux campaign against the fort builders. The Sioux leaders consulted one of the Thunder Dreamer societies, to tell them if they should attack Ft. Phil Kearny. [24] The society chosen

[23] *Ibid, pg.56-57.*
[24] *Freedman, The Life and Death of Crazy Horse, pg.60-67.*

16

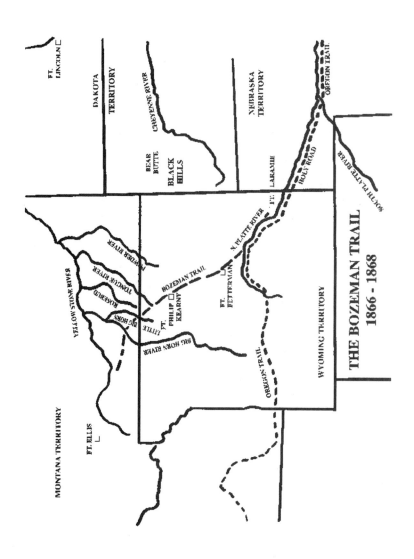

FT. LINCOLN

DAKOTA TERRITORY

CHEYENNE RIVER

BEAR BUTTE

BLACK HILLS

NEBRASKA TERRITORY

OREGON TRAIL

FT. LARAMIE

HOLY ROAD

SOUTH PLATTE RIVER

POWDER RIVER

YELLOWSTONE RIVER

TONGUE RIVER

ROSEBUD

BIG HORN

FT. PHILIP KEARNY

LITTLE BIG HORN RIVER

BOZEMAN TRAIL

N. PLATTE RIVER

FT. FETTERMAN

ORIGIN TRAIL

THE BOZEMAN TRAIL
1866 - 1868

WYOMING TERRITORY

MONTANA TERRITORY

FT. ELLIS

17

to look into the future was called Winkte. [25] A renowned Winkte noted for his power of prediction rode off into the hills for a vision tooting his eagle bone whistle as he went. When he returned he held out his hands and said, "I have 100 of the enemy in my hands". The leaders shouted with approval and began to prepare to attack the fort. Ft. Phil Kearny was located in such a position that no one could approach it with out being seen. So the Sioux warrior society leaders (Akitica Itancan) decided to wait until the soldiers came out for food, water, or firewood. On a wintry day a group of woodcutters left the fort to gather firewood. The Sioux, who had now joined forces with the Cheyenne and Arapaho, sent a small force of warriors to attack the woodcutters. The bulk of their warriors waited for reinforcements that were sure to come out of the fort to rescue the woodcutters. Crazy Horse was selected to lead a group of warriors to decoy the soldiers when they came out of the fort to help the woodcutters. Captain William Fetterman was selected to lead the reinforcement troops. Captain Fetterman had boasted, "Give me a hundred troops and I'll clean out the entire Sioux

---

[25] *Author's Note: The Winkte were a society of men that dressed and acted as women. The word Win-kte when translated into English means, "to kill the woman". In psychology there exists a concept called reverse psychology. In this concept if you want a certain thing to occur you do the opposite. In order to kill the woman you allow the woman to exist, Hence Winkte. In psychological terms the woman within is known as the anima. People with these traits are thought to have the ability to connect the other side, thus providing them the power of prophecy.*

nation". As he rode out of the fort Crazy Horse appeared with 10 men and successfully decoyed Fettermen into chasing them. As Fettermen chased Crazy Horse over the hill out of sight of the fort, Crazy Horse suddenly turned his horse around and with hundreds of warriors coming out of the surrounding hills, they attacked the soldiers killing Fettermen and everyone of his troops. Many horses and weapons were captured. The Winkte's vision was fulfilled. However, the forts remained, and the fight over the Bozeman Trail soon became a stalemate. [26]

---

[26] *Ibid, pg.66-70. Author's Note: Captured arms were used against the U.S. Army*

IRON HORSE 1867-68

General William Tecumseh Sherman, famous for his scorched earth policy on his march to Atlanta during the U.S. Civil War, decided to do the same against the plains Indians. [27] He reasoned that as long as the plains Indians had the buffalo they couldn't be subdued. So he encouraged the railroad people to establish a railroad across the plains, often providing soldiers to help them. Once completed, the transcontinental railroad led to the killing of thousands of buffalo by trophy hunters, some of which didn't even leave the train to kill buffalo. [28] The railroad also split the great American buffalo herd into two smaller herds, the northern plains herd and the southern plains herd. [29] This two pronged effort by General Sherman sought to subdue the plains Indians, one by getting rid of their food supply and the other by forcibly establishing forts across their land. But their forts became too expensive to operate.

---

[27] H.P. Howard, pg.5.
[28] McMurtry, Crazy Horse, pg.62-63, pg.73.
[29] Author's Note: The great American buffalo herd being split in two herds also caused some tribes that followed them to split into northern and southern groups. The Cheyenne, the Arapaho and for a time the Sioux had split. The Sichangu band of the Sioux had been following the southern herd, but eventually turned back

FT. LARAMIE TREATY 1868

With the forts under siege, it became clear that the government had to make peace. The result was the Ft. Laramie Treaty of 1868; Red Cloud stated that before he signed the treaty the forts had to come down. But Red Cloud was only a warrior society chief; he was not a civil society chief. The lead civil society chief was old Man Afraid. Not until after old Man Afraid arrived and began treaty negotiations did the government agree to close the forts and reserve the Power River country as their hunting grounds. Having approved the treaty the Sioux quickly went out and burned down the abandoned forts. But the Sioux had been mislead into thinking that the boundary of their new reservation was the Missouri River on the east, Platte River on the south, the Big Horn Mountains on the west and the Yellowstone River on the North. Actually the land west of the Black Hills was reserved only for hunting trips. So the Teton Sioux unknowingly had lost their beloved Powder River hunting grounds. [30]

---

30 *Ibid, pg.66-67.*

Ft. Laramie Treaty - 1868 Reservation Boundary

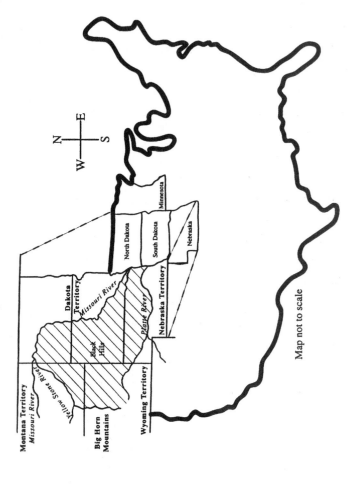

Montana Territory
Missouri River
Yellow Stone River
Big Horn Mountains
Black Hills
Wyoming Territory
Dakota Territory
Missouri River
Plate River
North Dakota
South Dakota
Nebraska Territory
Nebraska
Minnesota

N
E
S
W

Map not to scale

SHOT BY NO WATER — 1871

The Teton Sioux are descendants from an old matriarchy society. This society held the custom that a woman had the right to choose her own partner. [31] One night while her husband No Water was on a buffalo hunt, Black Buffalo Woman took her children to her parents and decided to elope with Crazy Horse. Crazy Horse was over joyed. At last he was with the love of his life. When No Water returned from the hunt and learned what had happened he took a pistol and went looking for them. Several days later he found Crazy Horse's lone tipi far from camp. He burst into the tipi shooting Crazy Horse in the face. Black Buffalo Woman ran off into the night and No Water went home leaving Crazy Horse for dead. But Crazy Horse was only wounded; the bullet had only creased his face. When healed it left a scar across Crazy Horse's cheek. When the Civil Society elders learned of Crazy Horse's actions they were appalled because Crazy Horse as a Shirtwearer had sworn to be a good example to other members of the band. After much discussion the elders decided to take away Crazy Horse's shirt. Black Buffalo Woman was eventually persuaded to return to No Water. No Water gave Crazy Horse his best horse as a peace offering, Crazy Horse accepted with conditions

31 Ross, *Keeper of the Female Medicine Bundle,* pg.226-230.

that no harm come to Black Buffalo Woman. Black Buffalo Woman's next child was light skinned. [32]

Soon after the scandalous affair Crazy Horse was talked into taking a wife by his friends. He married Black Shawl Woman, and one year later they had a daughter named They Are Afraid of Her. [33]

Crazy Horse took a second wife a few years later who was half-French. Her name was Nellie Larabee aka Ella Laverie. [34]

[32] McMurtry, *Crazy Horse*, pg.69-72.
[33] Freedman, *The Life and Death of Crazy Horse*, pg.87.
[34] McMurtry, *Crazy Horse*, pg.73. *Author's Note: Laverie is a french word meaning a place to wash.*

A tentative genealogy of Crazy Horse

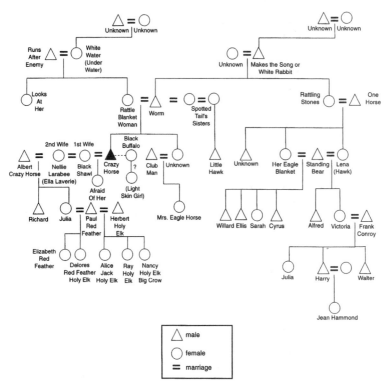

*Complete chart can be found in Appendix A.

25

FIGHT ON THE YELLOWSTONE — 1872

The Northern Pacific railroad was moving into Montana Territory from the east. The U.S. army on orders from above sent several hundred soldiers up the Yellowstone River into eastern Montana to provide protection for railroad workers. The railroad people clearly understood, that according to the Ft. Laramie Treaty of 1868, this was Sioux Country and the Sioux would not take kindly to them being there. Sitting Bull and Crazy Horse led a large war party against these soldiers. The military was well equipped, having recently received repeater rifles. Crazy Horse's attack failed to rout the soldiers,[35] but the soldiers and the railroad workers had enough. They turned around and went back east. The following spring the Northern Pacific people with an army escort commanded by George Armstrong Custer started west along the Yellowstone River again. Sioux and Cheyenne warriors decided to run off the soldiers horse herd. They caught the soldiers literally sleeping. The warriors had no intention of fighting until one of the Cheyenne recognized Custer with his long blond hair. The Cheyenne immediately turned to attack, followed by the Sioux. Custer held his own, then immediately fell back. The warriors disengaged the fight, happy to have many soldier horses. [36]

[35] Freedman, *The Life and Death of Crazy Horse, pg.88-89.*
[36] McMurtry, *Crazy Horse, pg.76. Author's Note: The Cheyenne hated Custer because Custer had brutally killed the Cheyenne Black Kettle and his people in 1868.*

THIEVES ROAD — 1874

For years there were rumors of gold in the Black Hills, but the Black Hills belonged to the Sioux as verified by the Ft. Laramie Treaty of 1868. White miners began demanding the government open the Black Hills for prospecting. So General Philip Sheridan sent George Custer with an expedition of men into the hills to see if there was gold. Gold was detected and Custer sent his scout Charley Reynolds to Ft. Laramie to announce the discovery. Right away gold hungry whitemen stampeded into the Black Hills in direct violation of the Ft. Laramie Treaty. The soldiers were ordered to stop all miners from entering the reservation, but none really made any attempts to enforce the order. By the time the Sioux realized what had happened, their sacred Black Hills was swarming with greedy whitemen. Now the Sioux began to call Custer, Chief of the Thieves and his route to the Black Hills, "The Thieves Road". Crazy Horse and other leaders sent out war parties to harass the miners. The miners had heavily armed themselves and would fight to the death for this yellow metal called gold. It soon became obvious that the whiteman didn't care about the law and would not leave. The government now had to find a way to get the Black Hills away from the Sioux. [37]

---

[37] Freedman, *The Life and Death of Crazy Horse*, pg.93-94.

FIGHT WITH 3 STARS — 1876

The U.S. Government came up with a treaty plan to buy the Black Hills from the Indians for three million dollars. Crazy Horse's friend Little Big Man threatened to shoot anyone who signed the treaty. Crazy Horse never attended any treaty meetings himself. Someone thought he had sent Little Big Man to the meeting. The chiefs refused to sell the Black Hills. The government returned to Washington D.C. blaming the Powder River Sioux for the breakdown in negotiations.[38] President Grant met with his military advisors about the situation and a plan was formulated. The plan was to send word to the Indians living in the Powder River hunting grounds to return to their agencies by January 31, 1876 or they would be declared hostiles and the soldiers would be sent out to arrest them.[39] When the deadline passed the military sent General George Crook to round them up. He wore one star on each shoulder and one star on his hat, so the Sioux called him "Three Stars". Three Stars found a camp of friendly Indians moving to the agency. He attacked early in the morning while the temperature was 40 below zero. Most of the Indians fled up a steep hillside, rallied and counter attacked. The soldiers then made a rapid retreat up the Powder River to join General Crook's main force. The Indians

[38] McMurtry, Crazy Horse, pg.82-85.
[39] Freedman, The Life and Death of Crazy Horse, pg.101-102.

suffered fewer casualties than the soldiers with only two dead. But they had lost most of their possessions and food. These friendly Sioux and Cheyenne now became bitter enemies of the soldiers and they turned north to rejoin Crazy Horse. Now began the great coming together of Indian people. [40]

40 Ibid, pg.103-105.

BIG FIGHT AT GREASY GRASS — 1876 [41]

Runners were sent to the agencies asking the reservation Indians to join them. By May of 1876, half of the agency Indians had left to join the so-called hostiles. The leaders Crazy Horse, Sitting Bull, Gall, Crow King, Spotted Eagle, Touch the Clouds, along with Two Moons, Old Bear of the Cheyenne, and Inkpaduta of the Santee [42], all leaders agreed not to attack the soldiers, but if they were attacked they would then fight. The Powder River encampment grew so large, that they had to move every few days to find new grass for their horses. In June the Hunkpapa held their annual Sun Dance, Sitting Bull himself participated and received a vision. His vision showed hundreds of soldiers falling upside down into the Indian camp. On June 16, Cheyenne scouts reported Three Stars marching up from the south. Immediately an emergency council was held, the leaders decided to attack Three Stars. Crazy Horse rode at the head of 1,500 Sioux and Cheyenne warriors. They attacked at dawn, General Crooks 1,000 man force became scattered and they never could form an effective battle line. [43] As the day closed the Indians left the field, Crook having lost almost fifty men and having

---

[41] Author's Note: In the summer the grass in the Little BigHorn valley, has a shiny appearance. Hence the Lakota called the river Peji Sla Wakpa "Greasy Grass River".

[42] Sandoz, Crazy Horse, Strange Man of the Oglala, pg.311.

some thirty wounded, accepted his Indian scout advice and marched back to his base camp. The Indians under Crazy Horse claimed victory. [44] The Indian encampment grew so large it had to move again. This time to Greasy Grass known to the whiteman as the Little Big Horn. The camp became two miles long and three quarters of a mile wide. It was thought to be the largest encampment of Indians ever assembled on the plains. [45] The Sioux and Cheyenne scouts had seen soldiers coming from the northwest (Colonel John Gibbon) and soldiers coming from the northeast (Colonel George Custer). The Indians felt that their camp was so large that to attack them would be fool hardy, even suicidal. So they were surprised when the shooting started on the 25th of June. Custer had sent Major Reno to attack the camp from the southeast. Reno was soon pushed back to a bluff across the Little Big Horn River. Next Custer attacked from the east. Crazy Horse, leading over 1,000 warriors, out flanked Custer from the north. Soon Custer was completely surrounded. Even though Custer had superior weapons he was shortly overrun by the Indians. Not a soul in Custer's command survived. Sitting Bull's vision was fulfilled. It was a great

---

[44] McMurtry, *Crazy Horse*, pg.94-95.
[45] *Ibid, pg.84. Author's Note: Michno in his book Lakota Noon thought Black Kettle's village on the Washita River in 1868 was analogous to the village on the Little BigHorn River in 1876.*

victory for the Sioux, Cheyenne and Arapaho. [46] Over 265 soldiers were dead and approximately 20 warriors had died. [47] That night many victory dances were held and the leaders of the Indians met in council to decide what to do next. If they attacked Reno, they could destroy him too, but it was decided to break camp and scatter in different directions. [48] This they did on the 26th of June, but not before they set the prairie on fire to hide their trail. [49] With the Custer massacre the government now had an excuse to steal the Black Hills. This they did through a treaty called the Black Hills Agreement of 1876. The required number of Sioux never signed the agreement but the government took the Black Hills in spite of the shortage of signatures. [50]

[46] Freedman, *The Life and Death of Crazy Horse*, pg.113-126.
[47] Michno, *Lakota Noon*, pg.281. *Author's Note: Death counts were probability less, because Indian witnesses may have seen the same warrior killed. Also, the death count did not include the women and children slain by the soldiers.*
[48] McMurtry, *Crazy Horse*, pg.105. *Author's Note: Among the Teton, any dance associated with war is danced is a counter clock-wise motion. This represents an anti-natural movement.*
[49] Freedman, *The Life and Death of Crazy Horse*, pg.127.
[50] *Ibid*, pg.130. *Author's Note: Signed by the Sioux on Sept. 26, 1876, ratified by congress Feb. 28, 1877.*

HANGING WOMAN CREEK
ESCAPE — 1877

The government wanted revenge for the Battle of Little Big Horn; they sent Colonel Nelson Miles after Sitting Bull and General Crook after Crazy Horse. Colonel Miles, called "Bear Coat" by the Indians, fought a few skirmishes with Sitting Bull, but Sitting Bull escaped to Canada as did Inkpaduta and the Santees. General Crook marched north with 2,000 men and sixty agency Sioux scouts led by No Water. While looking for Crazy Horse, Crook came upon Dull Knife and Little Wolf camped on the Powder River. Crook attacked in a snowstorm; the Cheyenne fled, leaving all of their belongings behind. The Cheyenne went to Crazy Horse, camped on the Tongue River, for help. Crazy Horse welcomed the Cheyenne, giving them food and blankets. But with so many people to care for, Crazy Horse remembered his vision where he was to put the needs of the people first. He decided to seek peace, he sent a peace delegation to seek Colonel Miles. As they approached under a white flag, Miles' Crow scouts shot the unarmed Sioux killing five on the spot; the rest rode off to tell Crazy Horse what had happened. Crazy Horse abandoned the idea of giving up and led his people away. Colonel Miles scolded the Crow for their cowardly deed, then proceeded to follow Crazy Horse to try and arrest him. On New Years Day 1877, Miles found Crazy Horse camped on Hanging Woman creek in deep snow. The soldiers attacked at dawn, but Crazy Horse held them off until the women could pack up, then the village fled to safety. The soldiers followed and attacked again, a week later the two sides fought for half a day before a blizzard stopped the battle, and Miles returned to his fort. [51]

---

[51] *Ibid, pg.131-135.*

LAYING DOWN THE GUN — 1877

Crazy Horse had gone out alone to ponder what he should do for his people, upon returning Crazy Horse now realized he must surrender for the sake of his followers. In May Crazy Horse with approximately 1,000 people sat down with Lt. Philo Clark to discuss the terms of surrender. Colonel Miles wanted to claim Crazy Horse's surrender since he did most of the fighting against Crazy Horse. But in the end General Crook received all the credit for the surrender of Crazy Horse's 1,000 followers. Only 300 were warriors. After laying down his gun Crazy Horse rode into Ft. Robinson flanked by his friends He Dog and Little Big Man. They began to sing peace songs of the Lakota. Soon his warriors took up the song, then the women and old folks joined in. Thousands of agency Indians lined the route, and they began to sing also. A U.S. military officer witnessing this said, "By God, this is not a surrender, it looks more like a victory march". [52]

---

[52] *Ibid, pg.138-139.*

FORKED TONGUE — 1877

Many agency chiefs were jealous of Crazy Horse's popularity, especially Red Cloud, No Water's uncle. [53] But U.S. military officers flocked to meet Crazy Horse, intrigued by the fact he was never defeated in battle. [54] Soon rumors began that Crazy Horse was planning to leave the agency and returned to the warpath. These rumors had been started by No Water and his followers. The Nez Perce people were fighting against the army in the northwest and the army tried to recruit Crazy Horse as a scout to fight the Nez Perce. He refused but the army persisted. Crazy Horse told the army he came in for peace, and if they didn't leave him alone he would leave and go north. The interpreters began arguing over what Crazy Horse meant. Scout Frank Forward said Crazy Horse meant to return to the warpath. Scout Bill Garnett said Crazy Horse only wanted to go north to hunt buffalo, as promised when he surrendered. With so much confusion going on about what Crazy Horse actually said, No Water's followers quickly ran to General Crook and told him Crazy Horse was plotting to kill him. Crook ordered Crazy Horse to be brought in by the Indian police which were under the leadership of No Water. [55] Crazy Horse

[59] McMurtry, Crazy Horse, pg.133.
[60] Clark, The Killing of Chief Crazy Horse, pg.36.
[61] Kadlecek, To Kill an Eagle, pg. 49.

fled to his uncle's camp, the Sichangu chief Spotted Tail. Upon arriving he told his uncle the truth, he had done nothing to violate the terms of his surrender. Spotted Tail agreed to go with Crazy Horse to Ft. Robinson, so that Crazy Horse's side of the story could be heard. Upon returning to Ft. Robinson, Lt.Lee from the Spotted Tail agency, who had been riding with Crazy Horse and Spotted Tail, went straight to the post commanders office and asked to see Lt.Colonel Bradley. But Bradley, having orders from General Crook to arrest Crazy Horse, sent four Indian policemen to bring him in. Crazy Horse thought he was being escorted to see Bradley. Soon he realized he was being taken to the Guard House. Jerking free, he pulled a small knife but Crazy Horse's friend Little Big Man, who was now an Indian police, grabbed Crazy Horse from behind pinning his arms to his side. [56] A soldier guarding the Guard House stepped forward and bayoneted Crazy Horse in the back. [57] Crazy Horse died in the early morning of September 6, 1877. [58] During his life he had lost his brother Little Hawk, his beloved daughter Afraid of Her, the love of his life Black Buffalo Woman,

---

[56] Clark, *The Killing of Chief Crazy Horse*, pg.33-36.
[57] *Ibid*, pg.143. *Author's Note: The soldier that killed Crazy Horse was named William Gentles. After the bayoneting of Crazy Horse, the army quickly sneaked him out to Camp Sidney for his own safety. Gentles died mysteriously seven months later; cause of death was listed as asthma.*
[58] McMurtry, *Crazy Horse*, pg. 139. *Author's Note: Also, Indian sources say Crazy Horse died in the early morning of Sept. 6th, 1877.*

his friends Hump and Lone Bear, his way of life, and many Oglala who didn't understand him. Now he had lost his life. [59] Crazy Horse's elderly parents took his body north toward the Badlands. The next day they returned without his body. (A short time later, Crazy Horse's wife Black Shawl, who was sick with tuberculosis, died.) His parents never revealed the location of Crazy Horse's burial, leaving his memory to remain an enigma to this day. [60]

HO HECETU YELO
"That's the way it is"

"Shortly before crazy Horse was arrested at Ft. Robinson, he had a premonition that he would be killed. So he told his followers if this should happen, 'Paint my body red and dip me in spring water and I'll come back to life. If you don't, then I'll turn to stone.' During the confusion and turmoil of his death, his followers forgot to paint him red and put him in spring water." [61] Many people feel the carving of Crazy Horse mountain is the fulfillment of his prophecy.

53 *Ibid, pg.141-142.*
54 *Ibid, pg.140*
55 *Ibid, pg.142-144.*

CHAPTER 2

FIGHT ON THE GREASY GRASS
(Battle of the Little Big Horn)

FIGHT ON THE GREASY GRASS
(Battle of the Little Big Horn based on the oral history of the Sioux, Cheyenne and Arapaho)

In the summer of 1876, the U.S. Army had orders to round up the so-called hostiles living in the Powder River hunting grounds and bring them back to the reservation. The army initiated a three pronged campaign; Colonel John Gibbon marched east from Ft. Ellis in Montana Territory. General Alfred Terry marched west from Ft. Lincoln in Dakota Territory; General George Crook marched north from Ft. Fettermen in Wyoming Territory. These three armies totaling nearly 3,000 men planned to meet in the Little Big Horn River country by late June. [1] General Terry was the first to reach the Little Big Horn area. Scout's reported lots of Indians on the Rosebud River. Terry dispatched Colonel George Custer and the 7th Cavalry to march south along the Rosebud, cut west to the Little Big Horn River, turn back north and rejoin Terry and Gibbon on the Yellowstone River. The plan was to catch the Indians from two sides. But first they had to find them. Custer was traveling lightly, taking only his cavalry and pack mules so he could travel fast. He knew from previous experience that if he wanted to catch Indians he had to travel fast. [2] On the eve of June 24th, Custer's scouts found a huge Indian trail.

[1] *Hardoff, Lakota Recollections of the Custer Fight, pg.10-11.*

Custer marched all night hoping to catch up with the Indians. Early in the morning Custer's Indian scouts confirmed a large village in the valley of the Little Big Horn. His regiment was sighted by several Indian parties, so now surprise was no longer on his side. He had to move fast he thought, if he was to make a fight of it. General Terry's instructions to Custer were do not let the Indians escape to the south. [3] Custer sent Captain Frederick Benteen with three companies to the south to cover any southerly escape the Indians may try. Custer then sent Major Marcus Reno with three companies to the west and north along the Little Big Horn River to attack the village from the south. Colonel Custer with five companies then headed northwest along the bluffs on the northeast side of the Little Big Horn. [4] Custer's Indian scouts had reported the presence of a huge encampment along with their enormous herd of horses. [5] Either he didn't believe the scouts or thought he could defeat them anyway. When Custer reached the top of Medicine Tail Coulee a scout reported to him that Major Reno had already attacked the village and was being driven back. At this point Custer still could not see the tremendous size of the village. He sent Captain Myles Keogh with three companies toward Calhoun Hill. Custer with

[2] Henckel, The Battle of the Little Big Horn, pg.10-12.
[3] Hardoff, Lakota Recollections of the Custer Fight, pg.12-13.
[4] Henckel, The Battle of the Little Big Horn, pg.16.
[5] Michno, Lakota Noon, pg.59. Author's Note: The horse herd was estimated to be between 20,000 to 25,000. My spirit guides have informed me that there was 22,000 horses in the herd.

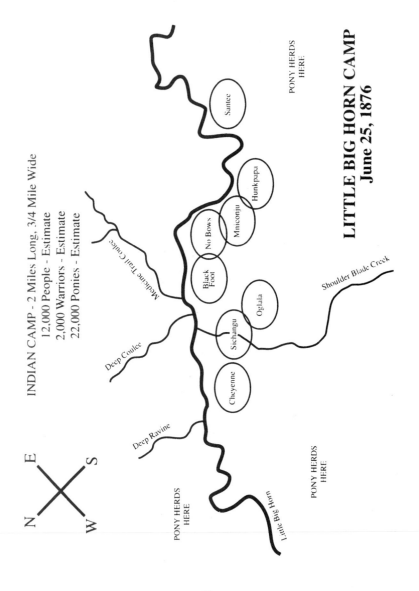

INDIAN CAMP - 2 Miles Long, 3/4 Mile Wide
12,000 People - Estimate
2,000 Warriors - Estimate
22,000 Ponies - Estimate

LITTLE BIG HORN CAMP
June 25, 1876

PONY HERDS HERE

PONY HERDS HERE

PONY HERDS HERE

Santee

Hunkpapa

Mniconju

No Bows

Black Foot

Oglala

Sichangu

Cheyenne

Medicine Trail Coulee

Deep Coulee

Deep Ravine

Little Big Horn

Shoulder Blade Creek

Captain George Yates and two companies went down Medicine Tail Coulee toward the river. He hoped that his presence in this area would draw pressure off Reno. Reno had crossed to the west side of the Little Big Horn River and started north along the river. Major Reno then attacked the village. [6]

It was about mid-morning when the attack started according to Indian sources. [7] The cry went out "the chargers are coming, the chargers are coming". Black Elk could hear the alarm being given from one camp to the next. Low Dog heard the alarm but did not believe it, because the village was so large no whiteman would dare to attack. [8] The first to face the soldiers attack were the Santee. They were camped among the trees along the river at the most southern part of the village. Inkpaduta and White Lodge, leaders of the Santee, immediately began calling their men to fall back into the woods. Inkpaduta was 60 years old and had been fighting whitemen since 1857. He knew instinctively what to do. He wanted his men to wait until the soldiers passed, and then they would come out of hiding

[6] Ibid, pg.106-108. Author's Note: My spirit guides provided the location for each tribe with the Little Big Horn camp.
[7] Hardoff, Lakota Recollections of the Custer Fight, pg.39-40. Author's Note: Official army investigation put the beginning of the battle at 1:00 far western time. For length of battle, see Appendix B.
[8] Michno, Lakota Noon, pg.24-25.

from behind and attack to the rear of the soldiers. [9] White Bull said he was watering his horses at mid-morning when he heard the alarm. He climbed a small hill and could see the soldiers coming. He jumped on his horse and chased his herd back to camp. [10] Antelope said it was beginning to be another hot day, so she and her friends went to the river to swim. Antelope was a Cheyenne, so when two Lakota boys came running sounding the alarm, "The chargers are coming", she did not understand them, but instinctively knew something terrible was approaching. [11] By this time, Major Reno's advance had reached the edge of the Hunkpapa camp, they began shooting at anybody, men, women and children. [12] Gall, a Hunkpapa leader, was sitting in his tipi when the alarm, "The chargers are coming", sounded. He immediately started north to get his horse. When he returned, his two wives and three children lay dead from the soldier's bullets. [13] Beard, also known as Iron Hail, was a Miniconju. His people were led by Hump, Fast Bull and High Back Bone. He said that Crazy Horse led the Oglala, Inkpaduta led the Santee, and Lame Whiteman led the Cheyenne. When they camped together they all looked to Sitting Bull as their leader. [14]

[9] Van Nuys, Inkpaduta - The Scarlet Point, pg.396-401.
[10] Michno, Lakota Noon, pg.25-26.
[11] Ibid, pg.24.
[12] Ibid, pg.51.
[13] Ibid, pg.38, pg.155
[14] Ibid, pg.29.

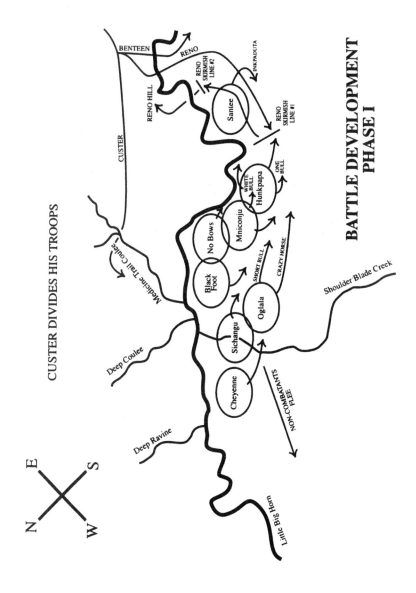

CUSTER DIVIDES HIS TROOPS

BATTLE DEVELOPMENT
PHASE I

45

One Bull ran to his uncle Sitting Bull's tipi to learn what he should do. Sitting Bull gave him his shield and told him to go out and meet the soldiers. Hold up my shield, tell them I would like to talk peace. But Sitting Bull was only stalling for time; his main concern was to get the women and children to safety. [15] When Major Reno reached the edge of Sitting Bull's Hunkpapa village, warriors started appearing from everywhere. Reno called to form a skirmish line. Old Indian men and women were now singing songs of encouragement to the warriors. The songs excited the warriors to rally against the soldiers. Reno's skirmish line began to bunch. [16] He was quickly becoming panicky, just then Bloody Knife, a scout riding beside Reno was shot in the head, spattering matter and blood all over Reno. The shaken Reno immediately called for a retreat. [17] As Reno turned he ran into Inkpaduta's Santee. Inkpaduta's ambush worked. [18] Reno temporarily formed a second skirmish line only to retreat in bloody panic across the Little Big Horn River. [19] In the mean time Arikara scouts were busy stealing Sioux horses. Many Sioux had seen what the Arikara were doing and charged the scouts. The Arikara wisely left their stolen horses and headed back east. [20] Red Hawk said the

[15] *Ibid, pg.39.*
[16] *Ibid, pg.56-59.*
[17] *Ibid, pg.87.*
[18] *Van Nuys, Inkpaduta - The Scarlet Point, pg.401.*
[19] *Michno, Lakota Noon, pg.87-89.*
[20] *Ibid, pg.57.*

Indians chased Reno across the river, many soldiers were on foot. They killed about forty soldiers as they fled to the top of a bluff. Here they corralled them into a small place. [21] Red Feather said he got a late start in the fight against Reno because he had been out all night with the girls. By the time he caught his horse and went to fight, Reno had already formed a line of soldiers. Red Feather said as we charged them, the soldiers took down their flags and retreated to the woods behind them. After a short while the soldiers rushed out of the woods only to meet Crazy Horse and his men. The Indians chased the soldiers across the river and up the bluffs. Red Feather said only ten men made it up the bluff and made a defense. Suddenly the women and children began shouting there are more soldiers on the north. Crazy Horse and the Oglala's left immediately for the north side of the camp. When they arrived, the Cheyenne were already fighting Custer and his men. We Oglala acted as reinforcements. We charged the soldiers twice, Red Feather said on the second charge I had my horse shot out from under me. [22] Gall had seen Crazy Horse, with a great many men, race to the north to attack Custer. [23] Short Bull who had been fighting Reno talked with Crazy Horse just before they left to go north, Crazy Horse told him, "There is a great fight

[21] *Hardorff, Lakota Recollections of the Custer Fight, pg.40-41.*
[22] *Ibid, pg.81-85.*
[23] *Michno, Lakota Noon, pg.68.*

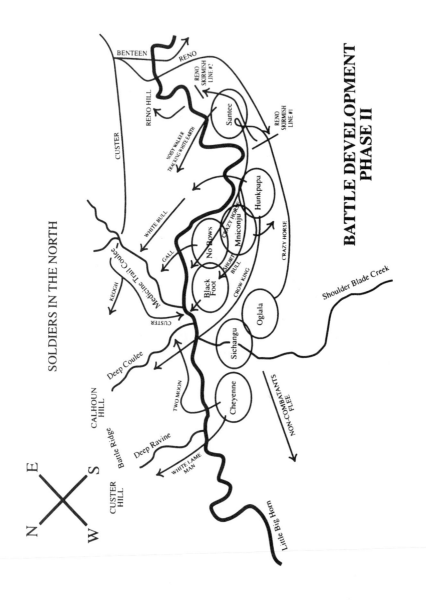

SOLDIERS IN THE NORTH

BATTLE DEVELOPMENT
PHASE II

coming over the hill," then both men turned and led their followers north. [24] Crow King followed behind Crazy Horse with many more men. [25] Gall stated as he left the Reno fight Inkpaduta's twin sons, Noisy Walker and Tracking White Earth accompanied him toward the north. All three men joined Crow King and went after Custer. [26] After Custer had sent Captain Keogh to Calhoun Hill he and Captain Yates went down Medicine Tail Coulee to cross the river. [27] Hollow Horn Bear said as the soldiers came toward the river, it appeared that they were hesitant to cross the river. [28] White Cow Bull said the soldiers did attempt to cross the river, but he and several other warriors began shooting at them. One of the shots hit a man dressed in buckskin in the chest. He fell from his horse; two soldiers rode along side and picked him up. The soldiers then turned and started up to the top of Custer Hill. [29] Now all of Custer's men held an elevated position. Keogh on top of Calhoun Hill and Custer on top of Custer Hill. Hump says that Custer went north and west, it appeared they wanted to cover any retreat. [30] Fox thought Custer went to try and cover the retreat of the non-combatants. When he realized there were too

[24] Ibid, pg.97-98.
[25] Ibid, pg.177-178.
[26] Van Nuys, Inkpaduta - The Scarlet Point, pg.402.
[27] Taken from the video, Custer's Last Battle, with Richard A. Fox. PhD.
[28] Michno, Lakota Noon, pg.131.
[29] Ibid, pg.119. Author's Note: My spirit guides informed me that the man dressed in buckskin was George A. Custer.
[30] Ibid, pg.132.

many of them he turned and then went on top of Custer Hill. [31] Wolf Tooth stated that the Cheyenne were the first to meet the soldiers at the river. [32] When the Sioux reinforcements arrived, together they attacked the soldiers and pushed them up the hill stated Ice. [33] Custer's five companies now held the high ground, a military advantage. But the Indians quickly started to flank the soldiers and then began to encircle them. On our first attack up Calhoun Hill we were forced back, too many soldiers, I counted four companies, White Bull declared. [34] Flying Hawk rode with Crazy Horse as they worked their way north to a place at the rear of the soldiers. [35] Two Moon circled around the northwest side of the soldiers, [36] with Crow King in front and Crazy Horse behind the soldiers, they were now completely surrounded. Two Moon attacked but had to fall back. [37] Next Crow King attacked and began to advance steadily. Many Blue Coats still on their horses suddenly dismounted, so we spooked their horses, said Crow King. Wooden Leg saw many soldiers ride toward Custer Hill then dismount. The Indians fell back briefly then Lame

[31] *Taken from the video, Custer's Last Battle, with Richard A. Fox Ph.D.*
[32] *Michno, Lakota Noon, pg.137.*
[33] *Ibid, pg.132.*
[34] *Ibid, pg.163.*
[35] *Ibid, pg.165.*
[36] *Ibid, pg.166.*
[37] *Ibid, pg.173-174.*

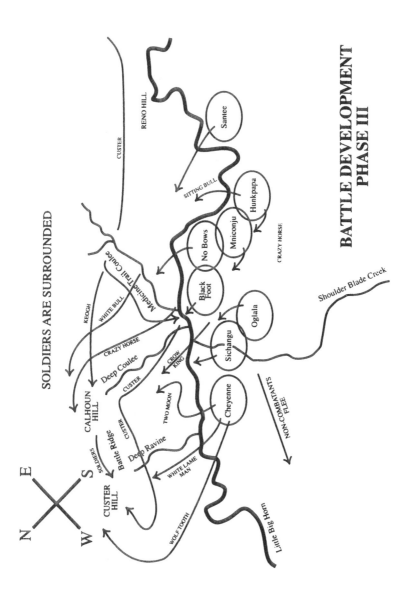

SOLDIERS ARE SURROUNDED

BATTLE DEVELOPMENT
PHASE III

51

Whiteman rallied the warriors for an attack. [38] Wolf Tooth spoke of how criers told all Indians to wait for the attack by the Dead Dance boys, and then they were to rush in behind them. As they attacked with many warriors it became hand to hand fighting. Lame Whiteman rode through the soldiers but was killed on the other side, said Wolf Tooth. [39] Meanwhile on Calhoun Hill, Crazy Horse and White Bull led a similar charge counting many coups as the Sioux swarmed over the Blue Coats. White Bull had his horse shot out from under him. He got up to walk when he noticed he was shot in the leg. [40] The attacks on both hills marked the beginning of a rapid deterioration of Custer's defensive line. He Dog noticed soldiers leaving both hills and running for the river. [41] Two Eagles said he saw about 12 soldiers run toward the river and jump into deep ravines. [42] After the battle the burial party found 28 dead soldiers in a deep ravine. The Last Stand was in the ravine, not on top of Custer Hill. [43] That night at the victory dance, the Santee Noisy Walker proudly showed everyone his

[38] *Ibid, pg.177-178, pg.196-197.*
[39] *Ibid, pg.197, pg.204.*
[40] *Hardorff, Lakota Recollections of the Custer Fight, pg.115-116.*
[41] *Michno, Lakota Noon, pg.219.*
[42] *Hardorff, Lakota Recollections of the Custer Fight, pg.146.*
[43] *Ibid, pg.32. Author's Note: the footnote, respects nothing states the battle ended in the ravine, also my spirit guides informed me that the Last Stand was at the deep ravine.*

prize. It was Custer's Horse. [44] The next day the besieged Reno was surprised when the Indians packed up and left the valley. They headed west for the Big Horn Mountains. As they left, the prairie was set on fire behind them, hiding their escape route and destroying food for any of the soldier's horses that might follow them. [45]

[44] Michno, Lakota Noon, pg.290.
[45] Henckel, The Battle of the Little Big Horn, pg.29.

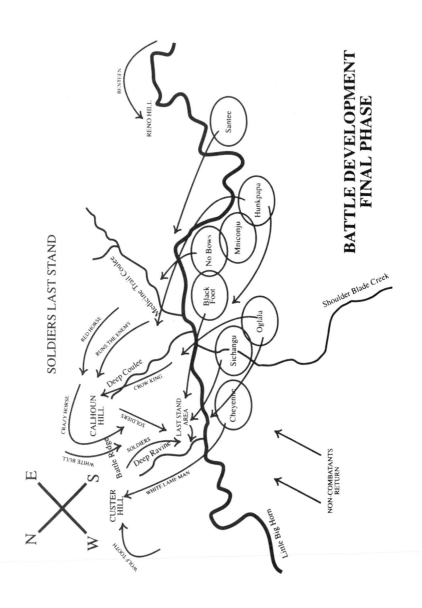

**BATTLE DEVELOPMENT
FINAL PHASE**

SOLDIERS LAST STAND

Santee

Hunkpapa

Miniconju

No Bows

Black Foot

Oglala

Sichangu

Cheyenne

BENTEEN

RENO HILL

Medicine Trail Coulee

RED HORSE

RUNS THE ENEMY

Deep Coulee

CROW KING

CRAZY HORSE

CALHOUN HILL

WHITE BULL

Battle Ridge

SOLDIERS

SOLDIERS

LAST STAND AREA

Deep Ravine

CUSTER HILL

WHITE LAME MAN

WOLF TOOTH

Little Big Horn

Shoulder Blade Creek

NON-COMBATANTS RETURN

N E S W

ORAL HISTORY WAS BY THE FOLLOWING MEN AND THEIR TRIBAL AFFILIATION

CHEYENNE
ANTELOPE
LAME WHITEMAN
ICE
WOLF TOOTH
TWO MOON
WOODEN LEG

MINICONJU (SIOUX)
BEARD
HUMP
FAST BULL
HIGH BACK BONE

OGLALA (SIOUX)
BLACK ELK
RED HAWK
RED FEATHER
WHITE COW BULL
FLYING HAWK
HE DOG
SHORT BULL

ARAPAHO
WATERMAN

SANTEE (SIOUX)
INKPADUTA
NOISY WALKING
TRACKING WHITE EARTH
WHITE LODGE

HUNKPAPA (SIOUX)
WHITE BULL
GALL
SITTING BULL
ONE BULL
CROW KING

SICHANGU (SIOUX)
HOLLOW HORN BEAR
TWO EAGLE

ARIKARA
BLOODY KNIFE

CHAPTER 3
ALL THINGS ARE RELATED

As a student of Astrology, I realize that the influences that guide men are cyclic. These minute influences can best be explained by the Sioux concept of Mitakuye Oyasin, "Everything is Related". (For a more detailed explanation of Astrology, see pages 153-162 in Keeper of the Female Medicine Bundle 1998, by A.C. Ross)

I learned that everything that has a beginning, whether it be a concept, a person's life, or even the construction of an object, can be traced back to the movement of God's heavenly bodies. Therefore, I decided to ask my Astrologer Mary Jayn to do a star map on the Battle of the Little Big Horn based on the natal or birth time of the Battle. Gregory Michno in his excellent book on the Battle entitled Lakota Noon, said there is evidence that the Battle started at 1:00pm. [15] Since in the 1870's the United States did not have daylight savings time, the starting time for the Battle had to be adjusted 1 hour in order to get a current computer print out. The following is the computer print out with accompanying chart interpretation by Mary Jayn.

This is a chart of an event, which is interpreted differently than a natal chart.

---

[15] Michno, Lakota Noon, pg.XI of the Preface.

Little Big Horn Battle
Natal Chart
Jun 25 1876
2:00 PM +7:09:51
Crow Agency
45N36 06 107W27 38
Geocentric
Tropical
Placidus
Mean Node

Compliments of:-
Mary Jayn
8527 West Colfax Avenue #208
Lakewood, CO 80215
(303) 232-8671

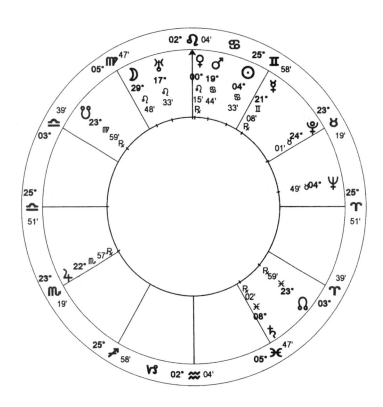

57

Because Libra is on the First House or the Ascendant of this chart, this is the aggressor - the U.S. Army. Because the ruler of Libra is Venus which is going backwards or is Retrograde [16] this indicates that the aggressor will not prevail nor win.

Because Venus is in the sign of Leo it indicates an aggressor who is proud, arrogant; because it is in 00 of Leo it means unpreparedness. [17]

Another meaning of a planet in an event chart which is Retrograde is that a similar event has happened before. [18]

The Indian Nation which was attacked is represented by the 7th house with Neptune in this part of the chart. Neptune is the planet of being taken advantage of, the underdog, those who have no power. [19]

Whenever an event is begun with the Moon void of course or at 29 degrees (usually) it indicates that the events will take a peculiar turn - very unpredictable and not anticipated. [20]

The attackers were inordinately intoxicated with pride and thought the outcome would be very different. Observe Jupiter sitting on the cusp of the second house

---

[16] Author's Note: Retrograde implies the energy will be nullified.

[17] Author's Note: Custer was proud and arrogant.

[18] Author's Note: Custer attacked a large encampment under Black Kettle in 1878.

[19] Author's Note: American Indians were not made U.S. citizens until 1924; therefore they were powerless at the time of the Battle of the Little Big Horn.

[20] Author's Note: Custer attacked therefore he thought he could win, but unpredictable and not anticipated results occurred.

in the death sign of Scorpio giving inordinate expectations of success. But Jupiter is Retrograde and in an event chart a planet which is Retrograde does not deliver. It falls short. [21]

Observe also that Pluto the death planet is in the 8th house (the death house) of this chart. The 8th house of this event chart indicates deaths of the aggressors. In addition this Pluto is sitting on the most malevolent star ALGOL at 24 Taurus - IN THE DEATH HOUSE. Most likely many deaths occurred through wounds to the throat and the chest. (Venus in Leo, Pluto in Taurus). This was a slaughter! [22] Jupiter in Scorpio opposed Pluto across the death axis.

The Nodes of the Moon are very karmic; they are destiny. [23] In this Battle chart, the South Node of the Moon meaning the past and connections with the past sits in the 11th part of the chart which means high hopes for the aggressor. This Node of the Moon is at 23 Scorpio 59 and is on the star Beta Leo which is "the persecutor."

Interestingly enough this placement of the South Node of the Moon from the Indian Nation's viewpoint lies on the house of creativity, and love. It appears that

[21] *Author's Note: Custer attacked therefore he thought he could win, but unpredictable and not anticipate results occurred.*
[22] *Author's Note: This explains Sitting Bull's vision and the premonitions of others.*
[23] *Author's Note: Karma is the law of "what you do to others, will be done to you". Custer had brutality killed Black Kettle and his people in 1868. Black Kettle was under a white flag of truce at the time of the attack.*

the Indian Nations through past accounts of the aggressor's activities realized that there was "no love lost" where the U.S. Army was concerned and regarded them as persecutors. [24] (the 11th house of the chart is the 5th from the 7th which represents the Indian Nations).

It is interesting to see some other heavenly bodies affecting the meaning of this chart. For example, the star Alpha Scorpius at 8 Sagittarius 00. The meaning of this star is "obsession leads to downfall." [25] The placement of this star is in the immediate future of the aggressor (the second house). In addition, in astrology there is a way to calculate degrees of the zodiac associated with certain meanings. It is interesting to note that the degree of the zodiac indicating the Part of Catastrophe is - also exactly at 8 Sagittarius 00.

To sum up these two meanings, the aggressor through miscalculation, obsession with being right and disregarding the rights of others walked into catastrophe. [26]

The Part of Spirit in this chart is 00 Scorpio 00. Within minutes, here the Moon of this chart will trigger this degree. Mary Jayn asked sarcastically did the Spirits assist?

---

[24] Author's Note: Manifest Destiny was a term created by the white man to justify their treatment of the American Indian.
[25] Author's Note: They were obsessed with getting the gold in the Black Hills; this led to Custer's defeat.
[26] Author's Note: Unchecked manifest destiny led to Custer's undoing.

My Astrologer told me that before she did this star map or natal chart on the Battle of the Little Big Horn, she had not heard of the Battle. She had heard of Custer but did not know he was involved in the Battle, of course she knew nothing of the Indians involved in the Battle. When I explained what happened at the Battle, she exclaimed this is the exact information she got from the Battle chart! In answering her question did the spirits assist? My answer is an unequivocal, Yes they did. Let us look at signs that have led me to this decision.

1. Sitting Bull, Hunkpapa Medicine Man; had a Sun Dance vision on June 5, 1876, he saw soldiers falling into camp, a great omen of victory.

2. Cheyenne Holy man, Box Elder, dreamed two days before the Battle that soldiers were coming.

3. After an officer's meeting with Custer the eve of June 22, 1876 Lieutenant Wallace told Lieutenant Ed Godfrey he felt Custer would not live long.

4. On June 24, 1876, the 7th Cavalry came across the Hunkpapa Sun Dance ground of June 5th, when Custer's HDQ flag was thrust into the ground. All of a sudden it fell over backwards all by itself. So the guidon thrust the flag into the ground a second time, only to have it mysteriously fall backwards again.

5. On June 24th as the Arikara scouts were examining the sweat lodge remains they discovered signs that Custer was about to lose a battle.

6. On the morning of the Battle, June 25, 1876, Custer's favorite scout, an Arikara named Bloody Knife predicted he would not see the sun set that day.
7. On the morning of the Battle, Oglala Holy man Black Elk had a premonition that a great Battle was about to happen. [27]

Now if you told these premonitions to an Indian of that period they would have known instantly to beware. I am sure that even today those Indians who are raised closest to their culture would have the same reaction. Most whiteman are not taught to appreciate their instincts.

Research done on brain hemisphericy states that each side of the brain is dominant in different modes of thought: The left is logical, linear, verbal, sequential, and masculine thought. The right is instinctive, wholistic, non-verbal, spatial and feminine thought.

My research into brain hemisphericy indicates that modern society and especially our school systems place stress on the modes of thought connected with the left side of the brain more than the right side. Consequently modern man is taught to place an emphasis on books and libraries as the source of all knowledge. By contrast, in traditional Sioux culture, any time a person wanted knowledge or information, he attend-

[27] *Michno, Lakota Noon, pg.33*

ed a ceremony and requested the information from the spirit world via an Iyeska (Holy man). [28]

So based on the study of astrology and my own actual experience in this type of phenomenon I would have to say yes to my Astrologers question on spiritual involvement in the Battle of the Little Big Horn. The position of the heavenly bodies on that day did determine the outcome. Custer died for the sins of the "gold-keepers". Indeed the influences that guide men are cyclic. [29]

[28] Ross, *Mitakuye Oyasin "We are all Related"*, pg.11-25.
[29] *Author's Note: The heavenly bodies are in constant movement, advancing 30 degrees every 2,300 years.*

THE RECTIFICATION AND ANALYSIS OF THE HOROSCOPE OF CRAZY HORSE
by Mary R. Jayn

THE RECTIFICATION PROCESS

The Rectification of a birth chart is an exercise for an astrological detective. One must visit the past and from the paths of the planets, select the year, month, day, and time of birth which reflect the potentials of the individual in question.

History records Crazy Horses' involvement in significant battles, meetings in Great Councils, his arrest and death. Many of these events record the month, day, and year. From these clues and from reports of his character and other pieces of information, a sense of character evolves and takes shape.

In this particular case, this horoscope must show an individual who would be martyred as a result of circumstance fulfilling his goal to preserve things as they are. It must show one who quietly communed with nature, who was spiritual, taciturn — yet a man of action. And, it must reflect a man who was his own person — the deviant one.

With these parameters a test chart emerges against which the chart is tested for accuracy. For example, using Solar Arc measurements [1] one can assess how the horoscope responds to certain events. Then, the transits of the planets are applied to the test chart for verification. From this assessment the month and day can be determined.

Using these main parameters and the information from Dr. A. Ross Ehanamani's spirit guides, I have rectified Crazy Horses' birth to be: May 5, 1840; 8:28:56 am; 43N54; 102W36.

HOROSCOPE ANALYSIS

With Sun in Taurus and Moon in Cancer this is a person whose main drive was to preserve the status-quo to gain security for himself and his people. This Sun Moon placement gives a stubborn streak within the character; one who won't yield easily.

With Cancer rising and with the Moon in Cancer, he felt responsible for actually feeding his own — which he did. Cancer rising gives an attachment to one's own family which was his people.

Pattern placement of the planets in Crazy Horse's chart are top heavy — the emphasis is above the horizon. This indicates that despite his choice of the quiet life, communing with nature in his own way,

[1] *A technique involving yearly movement of the natal sun as the basis, or increment of movement. This increment is applied yearly to every planet according to the time frame in question.*

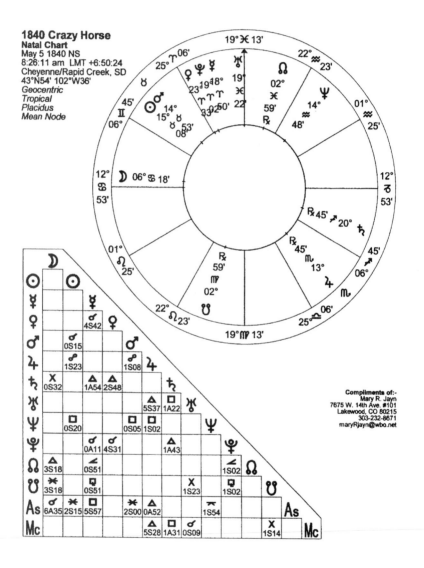

1840 Crazy Horse
Natal Chart
May 5 1840 NS
8:26:11 am LMT +6:50:24
Cheyenne/Rapid Creek, SD
43°N54' 102°W36'
Geocentric
Tropical
Placidus
Mean Node

Compliments of:-
Mary R. Jayn
7675 W. 14th Ave. #101
Lakewood, CO 80215
303-232-8671
maryRjayn@wbo.net

circumstances would deem otherwise. This planetary placement indicates victimization. Who would say otherwise?

This is a feeling individual. Note the Moon in its own sign on the Ascendant AND peregrine [2]. The feeling level, the attachment to family, and the need to feel secure within these constructs is emphasized.

One aspect (165º) from the Moon to Saturn in the 6th house indicates an obsessive need to take care of his family and he considered this his work. (Saturn is in the 6th of work and in the principled sign of Sagittarius).

Status to Crazy Horse was irrelevant. He listened to the voice within. His Sun, Mars conjunction in Taurus is square to Neptune in the 8th. This is ego relinquishment. Furthermore, the sign Pisces lies on the Midheaven of this chart — this is martyrdom.

To pursue his belief system more thoroughly, note that Uranus is in the 10th but very close to the Midheaven — its most powerful position. Uranus is in mutual reception with Neptune in the 8th. In other words, Uranus is in Pisces which is Neptune's sign. Neptune is in Aquarius which is Uranus' sign. A mutual reception emphasizes the importance of the planets. In this case, Spirit (Neptune) reinforced belief

[2] *Author's Note: No sextile, square, opposition, conjunction, or thrine to any other planets.*

(Uranus) and translated it into a defiant person.

This person emerges because Uranus is closely square Saturn — one who is defiant, one who resists authority. Historically, those born with Uranus square Saturn are those individuals who are in the teetering brink of societal change. These are the ones who pay the price of changing society. Also, Uranus on the midheaven gives the quality of humanitarianism to this "special person."

Although Taurus can represent an individual who could be taciturn, in this chart Pluto is conjunct Mercury which accounts for Crazy Horses' being a "man of few words." With Venus, Pluto, and Mercury all conjunct in Aries, Crazy Horse would say, "What you do, speaks louder that what you say."

Crazy Horses' death and the circumstances which surround it speaks eloquently from this chart. The fourth house — the end of things and of life — is ruled by Virgo in this chart. Virgo is ruled by Mercury which also rules the 12th house of betrayal and secret enemies.

APPENDIX A

A tentative genealogy of Crazy Horse

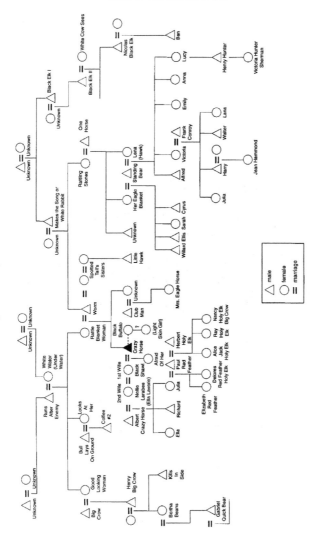

This chart was provided to me by Ben "Butch" Sherman.
His lineage is from Rattling Stones woman.
She was Crazy Horse's Paternal Aunt (Worm's Sister).

69

APPENDIX B

LENGTH OF THE BATTLE

	INDIANS	SOLDIERS
RENO ATTACKS	9:30 (approximate)	1:00 pm
SOLDIERS IN THE NORTH	10:30 (approximate)	2:00 pm
SOLDIERS ARE SURROUNDED	11:30 (approximate)	3:00 pm
LAST STAND	12:00 (approximate)	4:00 pm

Note: The Mniconju White Bull stated the Battle Started at mid-morning (9:00 or 10:00) and lasted until noon [1]
Official inquiry by the Army stated the Battle started at 1:00 pm, far west time, [2] and lasted three hours.[3]

---

[1] Hardorff, Richard G., *Lakota Recollections of the Custer fight*, p.40
[2] Ibid, p.40
[3] Michno, *Gregory F. Lakota noon*, p. xi

70

APPENDIX C

ART WORK

Drawn by Martin Red Bear, Oglala/Sichangu,
Professor, Oglala Sioux College, Kyle. S.D.

CHARTS

Drawn by A.C. Ross, computer enchanced by
Jonathan Canady, Sir Speedy, Lakewood, CO.

MAPS

Drawn by A.C. Ross, computer enhanced by
Jonathan Canady, Sir Speedy, Lakewood CO.,
Source: Bozeman Trail map
          Freedman, Russell The Life and Death
          of Crazy Horse, p.61
          Ft. Laramie Treaty- 1863 map
          Ortiz, Roxann Dunbar, The Great Sioux
          Nation, p.92

PHOTO CREDITS

The United States Postal Service has granted permission
to use the stamp image of Crazy Horse for the cover of
this book, and at beginning of the Crazy Horse Section.
The stamp image of Crazy Horse was copyrighted © in
1982 by USPS. All rights reserved.

BIBLIOGRAPHY

Clark, Robert A. The Killing of Chief Crazy Horse.
Lincoln/London: University of Nebraska Press, 1976.

Freedman, Russell. The Life and Death of Crazy Horse.
New York: Holiday House, 1996.

Hardorff, Richard G. Lakota Recollections of the Custer Fight.
Lincoln/London: University of Nebraska Press, 1997.

Henckel, Mark. The Battle of the Little Big Horn.
Billings/Helena, Montana, Falcon Press, 1992.

Howard, H.P. Crazy Horse - Tashunka Witko.
Pamphlet, copyright 1975.

Kadlecek, Edward and Mabell. To Kill an Eagle.
Boulder: Johnson Books, 1981.

McMurtry, Larry. Crazy Horse.
New York: Viking Penquin, 1999.

Michno, Gregory F. Lakota Noon. The Indian Narrative of
Custer's Defeat.
Missoula, Montana: Mountain Press, 1997.

Mullins, Eustace. The Secrets of the Federal Reserve. Staunton, Virgina: Banker's Research Institute, 1993.

Mullins, Eustace. The Curse of Canaan. Staunton, Virginia: Revelation Books, 1987.

Ross, Allen. Mitakuye Oyasin "We are all related". Denver, Colorado: Wicòni Wastè, 1999, 14th Printing.

Ross, Allen. Ehanamani "Walks Among". Denver, Colorado: Wicòni Wastè, 1997, 4th Printing.

Ross, Allen. Keeper of the Female Medicine Bundle. Denver, Colorado: Wicòni Wastè, 1999, 3rd Printing.

Sandoz, Mari. Crazy Horse - Strange Man of the Oglala. Lincoln/London: University of Nebraska Press, 1992.

Van Nuys, Maxell. Inkpaduta - The Scarlet Point. Denver, Colorado: Maxell Van Nuys, 1998.

Wilson, D.Ray. Wyoming Historical Guide. Carpentersville, Illinois: Crossroads Communication, 1990, 2nd Edition.

VIDEO

<u>Archaeology, History and Custer's Last Battle</u> with Richard A. Fox Ph.D.   Hardin, Montana: El Conejo Productions, 1995.

FIELD MARSHAL
ROMMEL

PREFACE

I had just finished "Jump School" Training to become a paratrooper in the Army Airborne, then went home on leave. My uncle Kenny asked where I was going for my tour of duty. Without thinking, I said Germany. In reality, I had not received my orders yet and did not know where my assignment was to be. After I returned to my post, my orders for final assignment had arrived and it read "Germany".

Thus began a new chapter in my life, the experience of living in Germany for 3 years. Upon arriving in Germany, I immediately wanted to learn all I could about the Germans. I even enrolled in a basic German language class sponsored by the USO (United Service Organization). After about a week of repeating "Das Rose ist Rot," I said to myself, this is going too slow, and I'm not learning anything I could use in everyday German conversation. So to learn the language I immersed myself in the culture. Although I never learned the German language completely, I learned enough to get around.

Many years later, after I became an author, I traveled to Stuttgart, Germany, to attend an American Indian Art Festival that was being held there. Our delegation was introduced to the Mayor of Stuttgart, Manfred Rommel. I asked him if he would read my book, Mitakuye Oyasin, "We are all related" and if he felt inclined to do so, please write a short endorsement for me. To my great pleasure he did. Years later, after I had written my book on the Life of Chief Crazy Horse, a German man having read the endorsement by Manfred Rommel, asked me if I knew about his father, the Field Marshal, Erwin Rommel. It was then that I realized I knew practically nothing about the Field Marshal other than he was known as the "Desert Fox." I purchased a book on the Field Marshal and began reading. As I was reading about Erwin Rommel's life, I became astonished at how identical the lives of Crazy Horse and Rommel actually were. In comparing the two lives, I found 36 identical items. So I decided to write a book comparing the lives of these two world renown warriors.

BIOGRAPHY OF FIELD MARSHAL ROMMEL

BIRTH

Erwin Rommel was born at noon on 15 November 1891, at Heidenheim on the Brenz River in the state of Württemberg, Germany.[1] This region was first known to the Romans as Alemanni[2] because this was the name of the Germanic Tribe found living there. The Alemanni were allied by the Suevi Tribe who arrived later from Northern Germany[3] and the two groups are the ancestors of the modern Swabians.[4]

---

1 *Rommel, The Desert Fox, by Desmond Young, Quill-William Morrow & Co., NY, NY. 1978. p.11.*

2 *Author's Note: Chamber's Encyclopedia states that Alemanni or all-men was a military confed eracy of several German tribes. The French adapted the word alleman to allemagne, which they now use to mean all Germans. Chambers Encyclopedia, Collier Publisher. 1890. Volume I, pp. 95-96.*

3 *Author's Note: German historian Jordanes states that the Germanic Tribes originally lived in Scandinavia and came south across the Baltic Sea into present day Germany in the Second Century B.C. History of Ancient & Medieval World, Volume 8. Editor Herk Dijkstra, Marshall Cavendish Corporation, Tarrytown, NY. 1996. P. 1021.*

German ancestral researcher Serbottendorff believed that the Germans originated from the le endary island of Thule. Thule Society, www.crystal links.com/thule.html. pp. 1-2.

The legendary Island of Thule was located west of Scandinavia in the Atlantic. The Vinland Map and Tarter Relation, by R.A. Skelton, Thomas E. Marston & George D. Painter, New Haven and London/Yale University Press, New Haven, Conn. 1995. p. 135.

4 *Short History of Swabia, by Harald Pheimer; web: http://www.mpip-mainz.mpg-de/-pliemer/. p.1.*

CHILDHOOD

A part of Swabia became the Württemberg Kingdom which had a proud militaristic history and distinctive German dialect. It was into this proud heritage that Erwin Rommel was born. His father was a school master and his mother was the daughter of Karl von Luz, President of Württemberg. Erwin Rommel was pale and often sickly as a youth.[5] His hair and skin was so pale he was given the childhood name of "White Bear." As a youth, he spent hours in the fields and woods. He remained a dreamy little boy until teenage when he suddenly excelled in mathematics, a talent his father had acquired. His every spare moment was now spent on his bicycle during summer and on skis during the winter. With his friend, Keitel, he began to use his mechanical skills to build model airplanes. The two friends planned a career in engineering.[6] But, Rommel's father advised his son toward a military career, so in March 1910, Erwin Rommel joined the 124th Württemberg infantry regiment.[7]

5 Rommel, The Trail of the Fox, by David Irving, Wordsworth Editions, Hertfordshire, England. 1999. pp. 8-9.
6 Rommel, The Desert Fox, by Desmond Young, Quill-William Morrow & Co., NY, NY. 1978. pp. 12-13.
7 Rommel, The Trail of the Fox, by David Irving, Wordsworth Editions, Hertfordshire, England. 1999. p. 9.

OFFICER CADET

In 1871, the many German states (formerly Tribes) combined to form a German Empire. The various German Kings, Grand Dukes, Dukes and Princes pledged an allegiance to the King of Prussia as being the Kaiser (emperor) of the New German Empire. The 1871 constitution established relationships among the various states, the Kingdom of Württemberg's Soldiers now formed the XIII Army Corp of the Imperial German Army. Local patriotism was strong, but now a national concept of "the fatherland" came into existence. The old Prussian concept of a throne being served exclusively by a hereditary, chivalric officer corp had been enormously modified. Nevertheless, throughout Erwin Rommel's life, he showed a wary scepticism over matters of social class within the officer corp.

When Rommel joined the officer cadet school in 1911, approximately 30% of the junior officers were of nobility (landowning families) which included the ennobled (those granted the prefix of "von" for distinguished service). Although Rommel's mother was "of nobility," he never thought of himself as such.[8]

While attending officer cadet school at the Baltic Port of Danzig, the cadets attended regular formal balls to improve their propriety. At such a ball, Rommel met Luci Mollin.[9] Lucie Mollin's father was a

8 *Knight's Cross*, by David Fraser, Harper Collins, NY, NY. 1955. pp. 8-10.
9 *Rommel, The Trail of the Fox*, David Irving, Wordsworth Editions, Hertfordshire, England. 1999. p. 10.

landowner in West Prussia. Italian in origin, the Mollin family had been living in Prussia since the 13th Century. Rommel fell in love with her at once. In January 1912, Rommel graduated as 2nd Lieutenant and returned to the 124th Württemberg infantry regiment. He and Fraülein Mollin wrote to each other everyday. Erwin Rommel had found the love of his life.[10]

---

10   Rommel, The Desert Fox, by Desmond Young, Quill-William Morrow & Co., NY, NY. 1978. p. 14.

WORLD WAR I

Upon returning to the 124th Württemberg infantry regiment at Weingarten near Stuttgart, Rommel drilled recruits for the next two years.[11] Having grown up in a Warrior Society,[12] he dedicated himself almost entirely to his career. He was a non-drinker and a non-smoker. Serious beyond his age, Rommel had little in common with the other lieutenants.[13] On the whole, Rommel had developed into a typical Württemberger; shrewd, business-minded, careful, with a hard streak in him.[14]

In the summer of 1914, Rommel was serving with the 49th Field Artillery regiment at Ulm when the outbreak of World War I started. Rommel quickly returned to his parent regiment, the 124th Württemberg infantry and on August 2, 1914, they marched off to war.[15]

The roots of World War I began with Russia. The Russians had driven the Ottoman Empire out of Europe and every German felt that Russian desire for more territory lay with their proxy, Serbia. Serbia had been opposed to the Austrian annexation of Herzegovina and Bosnia, so when Archduke Franz-Ferdinand of Austria was murdered during a visit to the Bosnian capital, Sarajevo, the Austrians quickly

11 Rommel, *The Trail of the Fox*, David Irving, Wordsworth Editions, Hertfordshire, England. 1999. pp. 10-11.
12 *Knight's Cross*, by David Fraser, Harper Collins, NY, NY. 1955. p. 13.
13 Rommel, *The Trail of the Fox*, David Irving, Wordsworth Editions, Hertfordshire, England. 1999. p. 11.
14 Rommel, *The Desert Fox*, by Desmond Young, Quill-William Morrow & Co., NY, NY. 1978. p.15.
15 *Knight's Cross*, by David Fraser, Harper Collins, NY, NY. 1955. pp. 19-20.

blamed Serbia (the assassination was carried out by Bosnian nationalists whose hope it was they would be joined by Serbia). A Serbian reply to an Austrian ultimatum was deemed inadequate. On July 28, 1914, Austria - Hungary declared war on Serbia. Russia joined Serbia, Germany joined the Austrian Alliance, France then joined Russia/Serbia. Then the British joined France. World War I had begun.[16]

For more than two years Rommel fought in the battle fields of France. In September 1914, Rommel was wounded in the left thigh while attacking three french soldiers. He was alone and continued the attack even after he ran out of ammunition. For this action he was awarded the Iron Cross, 2nd class. In January 1915, Rommel, fighting in trench warfare, crawled with his riflemen through 100 yards of barbed wire into the center of the French positions, capturing four bunkers. He then held them against counter attacked by a French battalion, then withdrew before the French could raise a second attack. For this action Rommel was awarded the Iron Cross, 1st class.[17]

From the beginning these exploits marked Rommel apart from the rest of the officers. He was always eager and anxious to act despite his small stature. He inspired his men with his initiative, courage, and acts of gallantry.[18]

It is without question that Rommel's willingness to

16 Ibid., pp. 20-22.
17 Rommel - The Trail of the Fox, by David Irving. Wordsworth Editions, Hertfordshire, England. 1999. p.12.
18 Ibid., pp. 12-13.

It is without question that Rommel's willingness to take risks and individual actions led to an increase in rank, (1st Lieutenant) and a new assignment. As the head of a battle group within the Württemberg Mountains Battalion, Rommel was given intensive training in mountain warfare. While on leave during the years training, Erwin Rommel slipped off to Danzig and on November 27th, 1916, married Lucie Mollin.[19]

After a brief return to France, the Württemberg Mountain Battalion was assigned to the Alpen Korp. The Alpen Korp was made up of men from Bavaria, Silesia, and Swabia. Rivalry among the officers of each German Province was fierce.[20] The Alpen Korp was shipped to northern Italy. The Italians had entered the war hoping to win back the Adriatic port of Trieste.[21] The Italians had caused a series of set backs for the Austrians near Caporetto, Italy and requested German assistance. The German attack began for Monte Matajur close to the Isonzo River Valley in October 1917. The Bavarians were to lead the attack with the Swabians protecting the right flank. Rommel was not interested in following the Bavarians, so he persuaded his commander to let him attack the Italians independ-ently. The Bavarians were held up, while Rommel, in the darkness of early morning led two companies of mountain troops across the Italian front. Then at

19 Rommel, The Desert Fox, by Desmond Young. Quill-William Morrow & Co., NY, NY. 1978.
     p. 17.
20 Rommel - The Trail of the Fox, by David Irving. Wordsworth Editions, Hertfordshire, England.
     1999. p.14.
21 Ibid., p.13.

dawn attacked the Italian positions capturing a Battery position with out a shot being fired. He left one company to hold this while he advanced into the Italian territory. His first company was then attacked by an Italian Battalion. Rommel quickly turned around and attacked the Italians from the rear. Taken by surprise the Italians quickly surrendered. Rommel sent word to his commander Major Sprosser that he had over 1,000 prisoners. Major Sprosser sent four more companies to Rommel. Now with six companies under his command, Rommel renewed his attacked into the Italian rear areas. Finding a road hidden from view, he personally led his whole force single file down the road which enabled him to get behind enemy lines. While advancing toward Monte Matajur he captured a ration column, some 2,050 men. Then after marching all day and night, at dawn, Rommel approached another group of the enemy. With only two officers and a few riflemen, he walked straight into the middle of the group and ordered them to surrender. Completely surprised, 1,543 Italians laid down their arms. On October 27, 1927, Rommel scaled Monte Matajur from the rear, capturing the summit with little resistance. During his attack, Rommel had been on the move continuously for 50 hours, had covered 12 miles in the mountains, had captured 150 officers, 9,000 men and 81 guns.[22]

The next day General Erich Von Ludendorff announced the capture of Monte Matajur by

22 Rommel, The Desert Fox, by Desmond Young. Quill-William Morrow & Co., NY, NY. 1978. pp. 19-21.

Lieutenant Walter Schnieber. The Silesian company commander received the Pour Le Merite (Germany's highest military award) for this action. Rommel complained to his Battalion commander Theodor Sproesser, who agreed with him but told Rommel to forget the matter. This disappointment only caused him to fight harder. Rommel's command was now moved to the Head of the Battalion and this Württemberg Mountain Battalion was placed at the Spear head of the 14th Army. Now Rommel's Swabians began a relentless pursuit of the Italians using the tactics of Bluff, bravado, surprise attack and rapid pursuit. His little force was remarkable in victory after victory. November 7th, he captured a mountain pass. Two days later he captures another. On November 9th, Rommel approached Longarone, the headquarters of the Italian Mountain defensive system. After crossing the icy cold, fast flowing waters of the Piave in cover of darkness, Rommel was attacked six times while at the edge of Longarone, each time he managed to withstand the attack. During this time he set fire to the surrounding house to illuminate the battlefield and prevent out flanking maneuvers by the enemy. The next morning Rommel decided to counter attack. Just as the attack began, hundreds of Italians waving all sizes of white flags came toward him. The entire enemy division had surrendered. Rommel had captured 8,000 Italians in one day. One month later he was promoted to captain and the Kaiser personally awarded him the coveted Pour le Merite. The citation read it was for breaching the Kolovrat line, storming Monte Matajur and the capture of Longarone.[23]

23 Rommel - The Trail of the Fox, by David Irving. Wordsworth Editions. Hertfordshire, England. 1999. p.16-17.

World War I - Rommel awarded Pour Le Mérite

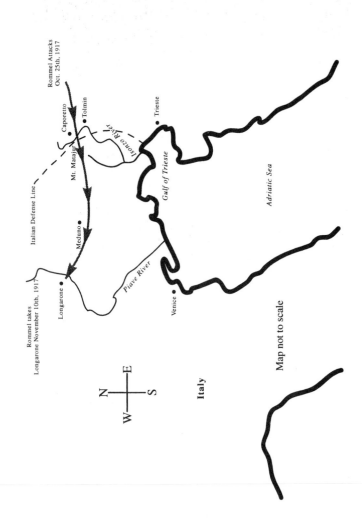

Rommel Attacks
Oct. 25th, 1917

Caporetto

Tolmin

Mt. Mataiur

Meduno

Longarone

Rommel takes
Longarone November 10th, 1917

Italian Defense Line

Isonzo River

Trieste

Gulf of Trieste

Piave River

Venice

Adriatic Sea

Italy

N
W — E
S

Map not to scale

VERSAILLES TREATY

The German people suffering greatly from hardships caused by the economic blockade of their country were surprised when the Kaiser announced the war must end. The German military in spite of being powerful and cohesive was simply out numbered by its enemies. Although Germany with its Austrian-Hungry allies had waged a series of successful campaigns in the eastern front, the Bolshevik Revolution in Russia was the cause for the Bolshevik's to conclude a peace with Germany in March 1918.

However in Italy, the Austrians who no longer had support from the hard-pressed Germans were being shattered by the Italo-British Army sued for peace in early November 1918.

On the western front, the German Army was being reinforced with soldiers taken from the quiet eastern front. The German Army began one final offensive designed to break the trench warfare stalemate and defeat the western allies before America could deploy their military in Europe. The German brilliant offensive came very close to succeeding, failing because of the lack of resources. An Armistice was signed on November 11, 1918, followed by the Treaty of Versailles in 1919. This resulted in the territorial loss of Alsace and Lorraine to France and the eastern provinces (including Prussia) To Poland. Also, unpayable reparations were demanded of Germany and a total disarmament of the Army, Navy and Air Force was dictated by the Allies. But a continuance of the Blockade against Germany beyond the Armistice produced famine and social unrest. This was an unnecessary humiliation. Thus, the seeds of resentment had been unwittingly planted by the Allies.[24] One could feel that it would only be a matter of time before hostility arouse.

24 *Knight's Cross, by David Fraser. Harper Collins, NY, NY. 1995. pp. 81-85.*

TEACHER/AUTHOR

Erwin Rommel was as demoralized as his countrymen following the war. He needed to find employment. Rommel's only training was that of a soldier.[25] Lucky for him, the Treaty of Versailles allowed Germany to have a tiny army of 100,000 for internal security only.[26] General Hans von Seeckt was placed as the head of the tiny army. His duty was to maintain internal order. To achieve this goal, he wanted well-rounded officers, university educated and versed in current affairs.[27] Rommel applied and no doubt his Pour le Merite, along with his reputation as a regimental officer helped him retain his career as a soldier.[28] He was stationed in Stuttgart as a company commander in the infantry. There he remained for nine years. As luck would have it, Stuttgart was close to Rommel's home, so he and his wife spent many hours in the country. Both were fond of horses and would ride as often as they could. In the winter, they enjoyed skiing and mountaineering.[29] In December 1928, Rommel and Lucie had their only child, a boy who they named Manfred.[30] Less than a year later, Rommel was assigned as an instructor at the Dresden Military

25 Ibid., p. 85.
26 Rommel - The Trail of the Fox, by David Irving. Wordsworth Editions, Hertfordshire, England. 1999. p.19-20.
27 Knight's Cross, by David Fraser. Harper Collins, NY, NY. 1995. pp. 89-90.
28 Rommel, The Desert Fox, by Desmond Young. Quill-William Morrow & Co., NY, NY. 1978. p. 30.
29 Rommel - The Trail of the Fox, by David Irving. Wordsworth Editions, Hertfordshire, England. 1999. p. 20.
30 Ibid., p. 20.

Academy. His lectures at this Infantry school resulted in the Publication of his first book, Infantry Attacks. The book was based on personal experiences during WWI. The book was an excellent manual of infantry tactics which contained many sketches by Rommel himself. The manual later became a textbook for the Swiss Army.[31] Rommel was the most popular instructor at Dresden. He never spoke more than 10 minutes without sketching a diagram for the cadets. In the 4 years he spent at Dresden, he was rated as a first-rate infantry and combat instructortor, constantly building up the cadets' characters. Respected by colleagues and worshiped by his students.[32] Rommel was promoted to Major in 1932 and in 1933, given the command of Jager Battalion.[33]

The word Jager translated into English means "Hunter." As commander of the 3rd Jager Battalion 17th Infantry.[34] Rommel was stationed in Goslar in the Hertz Mountains of Central Germany. He soon required all his men to have proficient hunting skills. Here in the forests with horse and rifle, he had two of the happiest years of his life.[35] Soon after arriving at

31 Rommel, The Desert Fox, by Desmond Young. Quill-William Morrow & Co., NY, NY. 1978. p. 32-33.
32 Rommel - The Trail of the Fox, by David Irving. Wordsworth Editions, Hertfordshire, England. 1999. pp. 21-22.
33 Rommel, The Desert Fox, by Desmond Young. Quill-William Morrow & Co., NY, NY. 1978. p. 33.
34 Author's Note: The Jager Battalion had originally been organized in Napoleonic Times as the King of England's German Legion. It was formed from Hanoverian German refugees who had been overrun by the French and fled to England. The Legion had a magnificent fighting record. So the Esprit de Corps of the Jager Battalion was difficult to match. Knight's Cross, David Fraser. Harper Collins, NY, NY. 1995. p. 103.
35 Rommel - The Trail of the Fox, by David Irving. Wordsworth Editions, Hertfordshire, England. 1999. p. 22.

Goslar, Rommel was promoted to Lieutenant Colonel.[36] It was during this period of Rommel's life that Germany suffered from high unemployment and militant unrest. Hitler and the Nazis came to power as a result of the turmoil.[37] But Rommel and the rest of Gen. von Seeckt's tiny arm, "the Reichswehr" were not allowed to participate in the political process.[38] Even if he was allowed to vote, Rommel probably would not have because he was virtually not interested in politics.[39] In 1935, Rommel was posted as an instructor at the military academy in Potsdam. He and his family lived close to the academy. He seldom mixed with the Berlin society and had absolutely no acquaintances among the Nazi hierarchy.[40] But this seclusion was not to last. In September 1936, Rommel had been attached to Hitler's escort at the Nazi Rally in Nuremberg. Hitler took notice of the excellent manner in which Rommel carried out his orders and personally congratulated him. Eventually, Hitler appointed Rommel to head his personal military escort. Instantly Rommel was among the Nazi elite. The Bloodless Annexation of the Rhineland and Sudeten Territories by Hitler impressed Rommel. Rommel attended Nazi indoctri-

36 *Knight's Cross*. David Fraser, Harper-Collins, NY, NY. 1995. *p. 566.*
37 *Rommel - The Trail of the Fox, by David Irving*. Wordsworth Editions, Hertfordshire, England. 1999. *p. 22.*
38 *Knight's Cross*. David Fraser, Harper-Collins, NY, NY. 1995. *p. 100.*
39 *Rommel - The Trail of the Fox, by David Irving*. Wordsworth Editions, Hertfordshire, England. 1999. *p. 22.*
40 *Rommel, The Desert Fox, by Desmond Young*. Quill-William Morrow & Co., NY, NY. 1978. *p. 36.*

nation courses,[41] but never joined the party, even after it was legal for soldiers to do so.[42] In November 1938, Rommel was promoted to Full Colonel and appointed Commandant of the War Academy in Wiener Neustadt, Austria.[43] It is speculated that Rommel's best selling book had a lot to do with his advancement.[44]

41 Rommel - The Trail of the Fox, by David Irving. Wordsworth Editions, Hertfordshire, England. 1999. pp. 26-29.

42 Knight's Cross. David Fraser, Harper-Collins, NY, NY. 1995. p. 119.

43 Ibid., pp. 126-127 & p. 565.

44 Rommel - The Trail of the Fox, by David Irving. Wordsworth Editions, Hertfordshire, England. 1999. pp. 27.

WORLD WAR II

After years of suffering (financial collapse, unemployment, starvation and near civil war), German resentment had reached the boiling point. Hitler had used this resentment to catapult himself into power. To further appease himself, as well as resentful populous, Hitler preached that every German should have equal status and deserved to share in the glorious German future.[45] After the restoration of German Territory back to the Fatherland (Rhineland/Sudetenland), Hitler began to seek additional German lands to be "liberated." First Austria, then on to Czechoslovakia.[46] The Czech president had signed an invitation to Hitler to put themselves under "protective care." Most of Europe was apprehensive of the communist threat.[47] Hitler used this to justify his protective care policy. He began to claim parts of Poland (where 2 million Germans lived). Poland quickly signed an alliance with the British. Then Hitler quickly signed an alliance with Russia.[48] With both sides "lining up their ducks," Poland, Britain, France, against German, Russia, Italy. These alliances made war inevitable. In August 1939, Rommel was promoted to Major-General and within a few weeks

45 Knight's Cross. David Fraser, Harper-Collins, NY, NY. 1995. pp. 106-107.
46 Rommel - The Trail of the Fox, by David Irving. Wordsworth Editions, Hertfordshire, England. 1999. pp. 29-30.
47 Knight's Cross. David Fraser, Harper-Collins, NY, NY. 1995. p. 134.
48 Rommel, The Desert Fox, by Desmond Young. Quill-William Morrow & Co., NY, NY. 1978. p. 43.

his safety.[49] On September 1, Hitler invaded Poland.
The second world war had begun. At Hitler's headquarters, a train code-named Amerika.[50] Rommel had
a front row view of the invasion. It was the first great
campaign in history which consisted mainly of tanks.
This Blitzkrieg or "lightning war" against Poland lasted only 3 weeks. The boldness and swiftness of the
invasion reinforced Rommel's fighting tactics of shock,
surprise, and constantly pushing forward into the
enemy's flank and rear. Rommel saw something else
that impressed him. A tactical means of mobility provided by the tank and armored vehicles.[51]

49 Ibid., p. 43.
50 Author's Note: Amerika was the name of a small village in Flanders where Hitler had won his
    Iron Cross in 1914. Knight's Cross. David Fraser, Harper-Collins, NY, NY. 1995. p. 103.
51 Knight's Cross. David Fraser, Harper-Collins, NY, NY. 1995. pp. 138-142.

GHOST DIVISION

Hitler liked Rommel, because Rommel was not the aristocratic class of officer whom he despised.[52] Hitler often asked Rommel for his opinion during important meetings[53] and often had lengthy chats with him on military problems. On one occasion, Hitler asked Rommel about his own career. Rommel replied he would like to command an armored division. Within a few months, Rommel was appointed to command the 7th Panzer Division.[54] Since all of Rommel's training had been with the infantry. He immediately began to saturate himself in the theory and practice of tank warfare.[55] Then came the German invasion of the west. On May 10, 1940, Hitler attacked into Belgium and France.[56] Rommel's 7th Panzer was under General Hoth's 15th Corps.[57] General Hoth was a part of Army Group A, headed by General Gerd von Rundstedt. Rundstedt's responsibility was simple, to provide the main breakthrough.[58] During the first few days' advance, Rommel's actions as a commanding general set the pattern for the rest of his career.[59] Rommel

52 Rommel, The Desert Fox, by Desmond Young. Quill-William Morrow & Co., NY, NY. 1978. p. 48.
53 Knight's Cross. David Fraser, Harper-Collins, NY, NY. 1995. p. 144.
54 Ibid., p. 144 & p. 151.
55 The Rommel Papers, B.H. Liddell-Hart, Editor. Da Capo Press, NY, NY. 1953. p. 6.
56 Ibid., p. 3.
57 Rommel - The Trail of the Fox, by David Irving. Wordsworth Editions, Hertfordshire, England. 1999. p. 39.
58 Knight's Cross. David Fraser, Harper-Collins, NY, NY. 1995. pp. 159-160.
59 Ibid., p. 164.

always rode at the very front of his Panzers.[60] At one point, he jumped into waist deep water to help build a bridge. This story did not take long to get around his division. Divisional commanders had no business being at the front lines, but Rommel never asked his men to do what he himself would not do.[61] Rommel advanced both night and day. At first, there was little resistance, but as he approached the River Meuse, the fighting intensified, Rommel was the first to cross the Meuse.[62] In 5 days, the 7th Panzer was far ahead of the rest of the corps. Rommel had caught French troops in their barracks twice, captured them and continued his drive. He had crossed both the Meuse and Sambre Rivers and pushed a narrow corridor, thirty miles long and two miles wide, into the heart of France. This quickness and boldness by Rommel resulted in 10,000 prisoners in two days.[63] Petrol trucks had difficulty keeping up with him. Once while returning to the rear, to bring the rest of the Division up to the front, his convoy of command car, signal section and two tanks were ambushed. His tanks were knocked out and he was surrounded for several hours before being relieved.[64] On two other occasions, fellow officers were killed while standing beside Rommel. Incidents like these did not hinder him from commanding in the

60 *Rommel - The Trail of the Fox, by David Irving. Wordsworth Editions, Hertfordshire, England.* 1999. *p. 41.*
61 *Rommel, The Desert Fox, by Desmond Young. Quill-William Morrow & Co., NY, NY. 1978. p.49.*
62 *The Rommel Papers, B.H. Liddell-Hart, Editor. Da Capo Press, NY, NY. 1953. pp. 6-13.*
63 *Rommel, The Desert Fox, by Desmond Young. Quill-William Morrow & Co., NY, NY. 1978. pp. 49-50.*
64 *Ibid., pp. 51-52.*

front. Once Rommel had walked through a hail of gunfire, to one of his Panzers, rapped on the turret and wanted to know why they were nor firing or moving forward. [65] Corps Commander Hoth recognized Rommel's effectiveness and made an additional Panzer regiment available to his command.[66] Rommel's Blitz Kreig (lightning war) was now firing on the move as it punched through the Maginot Line[67] in a matter of hours. As always Rommel was in the lead vehicle standing up and barking orders until his voice was hoarse as he continued on toward Cambrai.[68] He was now in France. He took Cambrai with almost no opposition and continued on to Arras. There he met the British Matilda Mark II, a slow, cumbersome, but abundantly armored tank. Rommel's standard weapons were useless against it. He soon learned that his anti-aircraft gun, the 88mm, had sufficient muzzle velocity to penetrate the Matilda's armor. So Rommel quickly took charge of his 88mm guns and personally directed fire at the advancing Matildas and stopped them in their tracks. During this bloody gun battle, Rommel's young Adjutant was killed only a few feet away from him. After the Arras fight, the 7th Panzer Division was ordered to stop.[69] Hitler had ordered the halt on advice from General von Rundstedt. Two days

65 Rommel - The Trail of the Fox, by David Irving. Wordsworth Editions, Hertfordshire, England. 1999. p. 44.

66 Knight's Cross. David Fraser, Harper-Collins, NY, NY. 1995. p. 167.

67 The Maginot Line, a French defense fortification, was billed as impregnable. Knight's Cross. David Fraser, Harper-Collins, NY, NY. 1995. P. 173.

68 Ibid., p. 176.

69 Rommel - The Trail of the Fox, by David Irving. Wordsworth Editions, Hertfordshire, England. 1999. pp. 46-47.

later the halt order was lifted. This delay had given the enemy time to escape capture. When the halt order was rescinded, the British were withdrawing to the Sea at Dunkirk.[70] On May 26, 1940, the British Government ordered their Army to evacuate from Dunkirk. That same day, Rommel was decorated with the insignia of the Knight's Cross of the Iron Cross.[71] Immediately upon the conclusion of this ceremony, Rommel threw a bridgehead across the La Baœsee Canal at Arras and jumped in his lead tank and headed toward Lille.[72] Lille was one of France's largest industrial cities and Rommel wanted to get there first. His early morning arrival on May 28 blocked the escape route for half the French 1st Army.[73] The remaining allies, totaling approximately 330,000 troops (two-third British and one-third French) completed their evacuation from Dunkirk on June 3.[74] The day before, on June 2, Hitler had called all his Division Commanders to Charleville in the Ardenne Forest to discuss the final days in the defeat of France. During the meeting, Hitler said aloud, "Rommel, we were all very worried about your safety, when you were on the attack,"[75] referring to the fast-moving forward exploits of the "Ghost Division," a name given to the 7th Panzer Division by the news media.[76] After a brief rest,

70 *The Rommel Papers, B.H. Liddell-Hart, Editor. Da Capo Press, NY, NY. 1953. pp. 34-35.*
71 *Knight's Cross. David Fraser, Harper-Collins, NY, NY. 1995. p. 189.*
72 *Rommel - The Trail of the Fox, by David Irving. Wordsworth Editions, Hertfordshire, England. 1999. p. 47.*
73 *Ibid., p. 48.*
74 *Knight's Cross. David Fraser, Harper-Collins, NY, NY. 1995. p. 191.*
75 *Rommel - The Trail of the Fox, by David Irving. Wordsworth Editions, Hertsfordshire, England. 1999. p. 48.*
76 *Knight's Cross. David Fraser, Harper-Collins, NY, NY. 1995. p. 191.*

Path of 7th Panzer Division (Ghost Division)

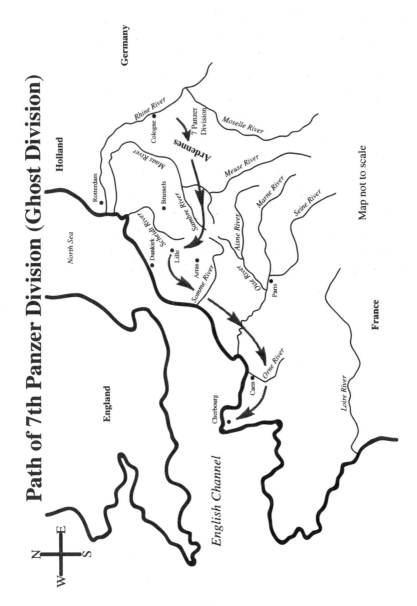

Germany

Holland

North Sea

England

English Channel

Rhine River

Cologne

Moselle River

7 Panzer Division

Ardennes

Meuse River

Maas River

Rotterdam

Brussels

Scheldt River

Sambre River

Aisne River

Marne River

Seine River

Dunkirk

Lille

Arras

Somme River

Oise River

Paris

Orne River

Caen

Cherbourg

France

Loire River

Map not to scale

N
W E
S

rest, Rommel and the Ghost Division were given a new assignment; stop the 51st Highlander embarkation from the Port at St. Valery. Rommel loved a challenge. First, he struggled across the Somme, then fought his way through the Weyand line. He traveled all night and the next morning had to put up with a small rear action guard, but by 2:15 p.m. had reached the sea. Rommel seized the high ground west of St. Valery, thus preventing anyone from leaving the harbor. General Fortune of the 51st surrendered on June 12th. Three days later, the Germans entered Paris. On June 17, the French asked for the Armistice. Meanwhile the 7th Panzer was pushing toward Cherbourg. The next day, Cherbourg capitulated to the Ghost Division.[77]

77 Rommel, The Desert Fox, by Desmond Young. Quill-William Morrow & Co., NY, NY. 1978. pp. 53-57.

AFRIKA KORPS

Following Rommel's exploits of that summer in 1940, his popularity grew tremendously. Rommel's friend, Kurt Hesse, the Army's Press Chief, wrote to him and warned that the publicity was creating enemies, as well as praise. In particular resentment, even hatred from among the German High Command. But, Rommel just brushed it aside as not important.[78]

In addition to Rommel's popularity growth after the fall of France, Italy's Dictator Mussolini declared war on Britain and France hoping to benefit from the spoils of war. Italy had colonies in Africa, the closest being Libya with one-quarter million Italian soldiers stationed there. Mussolini attacked the British in Egypt with a goal of seizing the Suez Canal. The Italian attack stalled and a British counterattack drove the Italians back to Libya. Mussolini called Hitler and appealed for assistance.[79] Hitler's "Plan Orient," which was to be a quick victory over Russia before the German Army was spread too thin, then a move from the Caucasus into Iran and Iraq, together with an offense from Libya into Egypt and from Bulgaria into Syria. Plan Orient was all about acquiring the mid-Eastern oil.[80] But Mussolini not knowing Hitler's plan had already invaded Greece and Egypt. Hitler realizing that an Italian failure would have side effects on

78 *Rommel - The Trail of the Fox, by David Irving. Wordsworth Editions, Hertsfordshire, England. 1999. p. 55.*
79 *Ibid., p. 58.*
80 *Knight's Cross. David Fraser, Harper-Collins, NY, NY. 1995. p. 214.*

his Plan Orient decided to send help to Italy. Hitler selected Rommel to head a Panzer division for the Italian aid in Africa.[81] Rommel who was politically naive knew nothing of Plan Orient.[82] He was a combat soldier, and a very good one. The German High Command who were jealous of Rommel allowed him little chance of success in Africa. Rommel despised the High Command in particular he considered Keitel, Jodl and Halder "Arm Chair Soldiers."[83] Hitler called Rommel to Berlin, made him Commander in Chief of the German Afrika Korps, briefed him and sent him to Africa with orders to establish a defensive posture. Rommel was subordinate to General Gariboldi, but could appeal directly to Berlin via Colonel Schmundt, Hitler's Army Adjutant, who was assigned to Rommel.[84] Upon landing in Africa. He made up his mind that his posture needed additional strategy. After air inspection of the area, Rommel's fingerspitzengefuhl (his instinct) paid off. He felt there should be a force at the Gulf of Sirte, not at Tripoli, the air inspection proved him right.[85] Next Rommel asked his Italian Commander to attack the British supply lines, Gariboldi said, "no." Rommel immediately had Colonel Schmundt communicate with Hitler's headquarters and received authority to go ahead. Within

81 Rommel - The Trail of the Fox, by David Irving. Wordsworth Editions, Hertfordshire, England. 1999. pp. 58-59.

82 Knight's Cross. David Fraser, Harper-Collins, NY, NY. 1995. p. 214.

83 Rommel, The Desert Fox, by Desmond Young. Quill-William Morrow & Co., NY, NY. 1978. pp. 65-66.

84 The Rommel Papers, B.H. Liddell-Hart, Editor. Da Capo Press, NY, NY. 1953. pp. 98-100.

85 Knight's Cross. David Fraser, Harper-Collins, NY, NY. 1995. p. 223.

Plan Orient

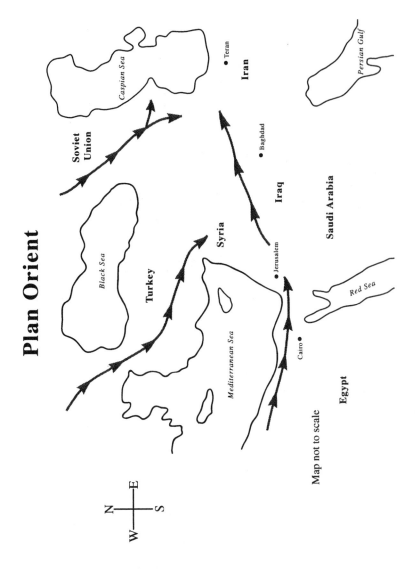

24 hours of landing, Rommel was on the attack.[86]
Rommel had been placed under Italian command for
two reasons: the majority of his troops were Italian as
was the majority of his supplies. Two days later on
February 14, 1941, the 5th Light "Panzer" Regiment
landed in Tripoli, within a few hours they disem-
barked.[87] Next was a propaganda parade for the
locals, where it seemed to be no end of the tanks.
Rommel had them go around the block several times.
Another trick to fool the British Air Reconnaissance, he
had hundreds of dummy tanks made, then mounted
on cars and motorcycles and driven between the real
tanks as they headed toward the front.[88] It took several
weeks for the 5th Light Regiment to complete its dis-
embarkation. On March 20, Rommel flew to Berlin to
receive new instructions. While there, he was awarded
oak leaves for his Knight's Cross for actions in France.
Then the High Command told him that the 15th
Panzer Division would not arrive until the end of May
and no more reinforcements would be available. [89]
Little did Rommel know that Hitler was about to
attack Russia and could not spare any additional
troops for him. Rommel was ordered to wait for the
15th Panzer Division before he advanced and then it
was to be only a limited attack.[90] The High Command

86 The Rommel Papers, B.H. Liddell-Hart, Editor. Da Capo Press, NY, NY. 1953. p. 100.
87 Knight's Cross. David Fraser, Harper-Collins, NY, NY. 1995. pp. 224-226.
88 Rommel - The Trail of the Fox, by David Irving. Wordsworth Editions, Hertfordshire, England.
    1999. p. 63.
89 The Rommel Papers, B.H. Liddell-Hart, Editor. Da Capo Press, NY, NY. 1953. pp. 105-106.
90 Rommel - The Trail of the Fox, by David Irving. Wordsworth Editions, Hertfordshire, England.
    1999. p. 67.

asked Rommel to submit a plan for the re-conquest of the Cyrenaica Peninsula for their review. Nine days before they were due to receive the plan, Rommel had already re-conquered the Cyrenaica. He justified his advance by saying te 15th Panzer Division had arrived. But the fact was that only the first ship had landed.[91] Upon arrival in Africa, [92] Rommel had spent the first weeks, acclimating his force to the 120 degree hot days and nights at the freezing point, the blinding sandstorms, rarity of water, miles of territory void of life and the effects of all this on his men and equipment. [93] So when he appeared on the Cyrenaica Peninsula, the speed with which he overran it was so impressive, that even the High Command took notice.[94] Rommel being a competent pilot did a lot of his own reconnoitering during the Cyrenaica conquest. As in France, Rommel flew a Storch aircraft while on reconnaissance and if he spotted his own tank columns moving slowly or stopped, he would drop a note that read: "If you don't move on at once, I shall come down! Rommel."[95] Speed was all that mattered to him. He drove his subordinates, General Streich and Lieutenant-Colonel Olbrich, relentlessly. When 1,700 prisoners (including one General) were taken at Mechili and 900 prisoners (including four Generals) at Derna, his only comment

91 Rommel, The Desert Fox, by Desmond Young. Quill-William Morrow & Co., NY, NY. 1978. p.74.
92 Author's Note: In The Rommel Papers, edited by B.H. Liddell-Hart, p. 100, Rommel stated that he had arrived inAfrica on February 12, 1941.
93 Knight's Cross. David Fraser, Harper-Collins, NY, NY. 1995. p. 228.
94 Rommel, The Desert Fox, by Desmond Young. Quill-William Morrow & Co., NY, NY. 1978. p.75.
95 Knight's Cross. David Fraser, Harper-Collins, NY, NY. 1995. p. 232.

to his subordinates was, "Why are you still here?"[96] and immediately ordered them to move out for Tobruk.[97]

During Rommel's expulsion of the British from Cyrenaica, he had attacked day and night for nine days, he had out-ran his supply more than once,[98] he used his fingerspitzengefuhl (sixth sense) to solve tactical solutions, as well as to orient himself in the desert. He was interested in the suffering of his men and he taught by example in leading his men. A general staff-trained officer, who had been observing Rommel during this time, stated: "Rommel is the most daring and thrustful military commander in German history."[99]

96 *Rommel's tankers were cleaning sand from their sand-locked gun turrets. Rommel - The Trail of the Fox, by David Irving. Wordsworth Editions, Hertfordshire, England. 1999. p. 76.*
97 *Ibid., p. 76.*
98 *Knight's Cross. David Fraser, Harper-Collins, NY, NY. 1995. p. 229-236.*
99 *Ibid., p. 240.*

THE DESERT FOX

Rommel was set on reaching Tobruk for two reasons: one, it was the only harbor in Cyrenaica and, second, he needed Tobruk because it blocked his supply lines.[100] But, Winston Churchill had ordered his British Commanders that Tobruk was to be held at all costs.[101] Before leaving for Tobruk, Rommel had acquired the use of two new words in his vocabulary. First: "Mommoth," which was the name of his captured British armored command vehicle that he would be seen in so often;[102] and, second: the name "Desert Fox," which was given to him because of his "fingerspitzengefuhl" (sixth sense), the uncanny ability to know when the enemy was approaching.[103]

Early on the morning of April 10, Rommel ordered the attack on Tobruk, having no idea of Churchill's order to stand and fight until death. Heavy British artillery fire, then a sandstorm, brought Rommel to a halt. He attacked again the next day, there was driving sand, but the attack continued, until his tanks were stopped by a large anti-tank ditch.[104] He was repulsed with large losses in men and tanks. Rommel got a "poke in the nose" on his first try to take Tobruk.[105]

100   Rommel - The Trail of the Fox, by David Irving. Wordsworth Editions, Hertfordshire, England. 1999. p. 79.
101   Ibid., p. 77.
102   Ibid., p. 81.
103   Ibid. Photo at bottom of last page of illustrations found between pp. 82-83.
104   The Rommel Papers, B.H. Liddell-Hart, Editor. Da Capo Press, NY, NY. 1953. pp. 122-123.
105   Rommel, The Desert Fox, by Desmond Young. Quill-William Morrow & Co., NY, NY. 1978.p. 76

Earlier some of Rommel's troops had bypassed Tobruk and captured Capuzzo, then Sollum. Both are east of Tobruk. Sollum is located just inside Egypt.[106] Rommel was a actually in Egypt, but he needed the port at Tobruk to bring in supplies. Before he could get resupplied, the British General, Wavell, was ordered by Churchill to attack the "Desert Fox."[107] The key passage into Egypt was over Halfaya Pass, which was on a very steep elevation that overlooked Capuzzo and Sollum. Rommel was holding the Pass.[108] May 15, the British counterattacked and immediately retook the Pass. Rommel had instinctively felt that British were about to counterattack, so he was ready.[109] It took only a couple of days before Rommel recaptured the Pass. The British fled in panic leaving a tremendous amount of booty (nine artillery guns seven tanks, and many trucks) and material that the Germans needed so badly.[110]

One of the great problems was getting supplies to the front. Most of what they received came from Tripoli, which was 1,000 miles from the front. The Italian Army was responsible for the transportation of the supplies. But, Rommel had no authority over them, so there was little he could do to speed up the delivery of supplies. Coupled with this, the Arab pop-

---

106 *Rommel - The Trail of the Fox, by David Irving. Wordsworth Editions, Hertsfordshire, England. 1999. p. 79.*
107 *Rommel, The Desert Fox, by Desmond Young. Quill-William Morrow & Co., NY, NY. 1978. p. 76.*
108 *Knight's Cross. David Fraser, Harper-Collins, NY, NY. 1995. p. 247.*
109 *Ibid., p. 252.*
110 *Rommel - The Trail of the Fox, by David Irving. Wordsworth Editions, Hertfordshire, England. 1999. p. 94.*

ulation made life miserable for the Italian soldiers, because they resented them for taking liberties with Arab women. To assist in his supply problem, Rommel sent a letter to the Italian High Command, asking them to treat the Arabs with respect, thus avoiding an armed uprising behind his front lines.[111] Another method Rommel used to help solve his supply problem was the use of captured or repaired enemy guns and equipment.[112]

In early June, 1941, as Rommel was riding across the desert in his Mammoth, all of a sudden he had a gut feeling, a premonition that the British were about to launch an attack. A few days later the British operation "Battleaxe" started. Rommel had only 95 real battle tanks, compared to 190 for the British. His front line was only half complete and had very little ammunition, food and water. The British advanced straight ahead toward Capuzzo and Sollum. Rommel maintained control of Halfaya Pass as the British advanced north.

His 15th Panzer Division met the bulk of the British armor at Capuzzo. After a furious tank battle, Rommel ordered the 15th to disengage and joined with the 5th Light Regiment moved around and into the British flank, lifting the siege on the defenders of Halfaya Pass and cutting off the entire British offense.[113] The three day battle ended in complete vic-

---

111 *The Rommel Papers,* B.H. Liddell-Hart, Editor. *Da Capo Press, NY, NY. 1953. pp. 138-139.*
112 *Knight's Cross.* David Fraser, Harper-Collins, NY, NY. 1995. p. 253.
113 Rommel - *The Trail of the Fox, by David Irving.* Wordsworth Editions, Hertfordshire, England. 1999. pp. 97-99.

PANZER III

Weight: 20 Ton
Length: 17' 9"
Height: 8' 3"
Speed: 40 Kmph
Engine: 300 hp Maybach
Armarment: 50mm Cannon
2-7.92mm Machine Guns

This was the "work horse" for Rommel's Afrika Korps.
The Panzer III held 5 soliders: Commander, Driver, Gunner, Gun Loader and Radio Man

tory for the "Desert Fox." He had out-maneuvered a
superior force. Rommel paid generous tribute to his
men and their equipment, particularly to the German-
Italian garrison that held Halfaya Pass.[114] Rommel had
taken 570 prisoners and knocked out 100 tanks.[115]
Rommel was then promoted to Full General and given
command of the entire Panzer Group Africa.[116] On
June 22, 1941, Hitler invaded Russia under the code
name of "Operation Barbarossa"; the initial step of
Plan Orient had begun. Rommel now realized why he
wasn't getting all he asked for in North Africa.[117] The
German High Command told Rommel that after the
Wehrmacht subdued the Russian Caucasus, they
would invade Egypt from the east. They told Rommel
that his task in Libya was to capture Tobruk first, then
examine ways to invade Egypt from the west.[118] So
Rommel flew to Germany to talk with Hitler personally. Hitler granted him all his demands for an assault
on Tobruk, but said nothing about Egypt. On the
return trip to North Africa, Rommel's plane developed
engine trouble, but managed to land safely. The next
day he was informed that the same plane he had flown
in on his return had crashed and burned, killing all on
board.[119] A few days later, Rommel, who was not feeling well, was diagnosed with jaundice. His doctors
advised a long rest. Rommel ignored their advice.[120]

114 Knight's Cross. David Fraser, Harper-Collins, NY, NY. 1995. p. 260.
115 The Rommel Papers, B.H. Liddell-Hart, Editor. Da Capo Press, NY, NY. 1953. p. 146.
116 Ibid., p. 153.
117 Rommel - The Trail of the Fox, by David Irving. Wordsworth Editions, Hertfordshire,
     England. 1999. p. 102.
118 Ibid., p. 102.
119 Ibid., pp. 104-106.

advised a long rest. Rommel ignored their advice.[120]
Rommel's new command was one-third German
and two-thirds Italian. The Italians had fought along
side him in the past and he had clashed with a few of
their leaders. But, now Rommel had six Italian
Divisions under his command.[121] As time was press-
ing, Rommel thought it was necessary to attack Tobruk
at the earliest possible moment. The German High
Command reluctantly approved.[122] The attack was set
for November 23rd. Rommel decided to spend his
birthday (November 15) in Rome with his wife Lucie.[123]
Upon arrival back in North Africa on November 18, he
learned that the previous night an attempt on his life
was made at the "Rommel Haus" in Beda Littoria by a
British commando unit.[124] That same day he also
learned that the British 8th Army was in attack.[125]
Rommel learned from a British soldier captured earlier
that the British offensive called "Crusader" was to
relieve Tobruk and push on to Tripoli.[126] The British
advanced out into the desert. It was unclear of their
next move.[127] But, being obsessed with Tobruk,[128]
Rommel hesitated. Then Rommel decided not to go

120   Ibid., p. 109.
121   Rommel, The Desert Fox, by Desmond Young. Quill-William Morrow & Co., NY, NY.
      1978. p. 88.
122   The Rommel Papers, B.H. Liddell-Hart, Editor. Da Capo Press, NY, NY. 1953. p. 155.
123   Rommel, The Desert Fox, by Desmond Young. Quill-William Morrow & Co., NY, NY.
      1978. p. 82.
124   Ibid., p. 84-85.
125   Knight's Cross. David Fraser, Harper-Collins, NY, NY. 1995. p. 278.
126   The Rommel Papers, B.H. Liddell-Hart, Editor. Da Capo Press, NY, NY. 1953. pp. 158-159.
127   Knight's Cross. David Fraser, Harper-Collins, NY, NY. 1995. p. 280.
128   Ibid p. 281

ahead with his attack on Tobruk.

The British sudden attack had spoiled his plans for Tobruk. Rommel lacked materials and supplies. He had only 260 tanks to the enemy's number of 924 tanks. So he decided to combine his mobile formations into a single compact force and fight the British one unit at a time.[129] For three weeks, the battles moved, forward and back, then forward again óver a fifty square mile area.[130] With the battlefields so scattered, it was hard to know who was where.[131] One afternoon Rommel was visiting a field hospital filled with both German and British wounded. As he walked among the hospital beds, the German wounded recognized him and began sitting up. It was then that he noticed the hospital was in British hands. Rommel immediately whispered to his aide, "I think we better get out of here." He acknowledged a final salute to those who had been escorting him, quickly jumped into his "Mammoth" and sped off.[132] Meanwhile in the very confused and scattered battleground, the British 8th Army led by a New Zealand Division, was about to break through to Tobruk.[133] At the same time, those in Tobruk had a tank assault trying to link with forces coming to their rescue. Rommel

129   *The Rommel Papers*, B.H. Liddell-Hart, Editor. *Da Capo Press, NY, NY. 1953. p. 158-159.*
130   *Rommel - The Trail of the Fox, by David Irving. Wordsworth Editions, Hertfordshire, England. 1999. p. 120.*
131   *Rommel, The Desert Fox, by Desmond Young. Quill-William Morrow & Co., NY, NY. 1978. p. 89.*
132   *Ibid., p.94.*
133   *Knight's Cross. David Fraser, Harper-Collins, NY, NY. 1995. p. 288.*

took command of the counterattack himself using the
Afrika Korps and flak 88mm guns shot down tank
after tank.[134] Despite being outnumbered, Rommel
won an astonishing comeback.[135] But, due to a lack of
supplies and heavy casualties, he couldn't continue.
On December 3, 1941, Rommel abandoned all ground
east of Tobruk. During operation "Crusader," the
German Afrika Korps had destroyed 814 tanks and
armored vehicles, 127 aircraft and acquired enormous
booty. They also captured over 9,000 enemy soldiers.[136]
But, the Afrika Korps had only 40 tanks left and very
little ammunition. On December 5, a message from
the Italian High Command in Rome informed Rommel
that supplies and reinforcements would not arrive for
at least a month.[137] In view of this, he decided to fall
back to Gazala and reorganize. Rommel's withdrawal
was done with his usual skill and speed. He arrived in
Gazala December 7.[138] In a month's time, he had
moved an incredible 300 miles to Mersa el Brega, pro-
hibiting the British from encircling him.[139] The British
8th Army settled back to reorganize. Just then, "The
improbable occurred: without warning Rommel
attacked on January 21st."[140] The British had been
fooled into thinking he was in a major retreat.

134 Rommel - The Trail of the Fox, by David Irving. Wordsworth Editions, Hertfordshire,
     England. 1999. pp. 122-123.
135 Ibid., p. 132.
136 Ibid., p. 135.
137 Ibid., p. 170.
138 The Rommel Papers, B.H. Liddell-Hart, Editor. Da Capo Press, NY, NY. 1953. pp. 171-173.
139 Rommel - The Trail of the Fox, by David Irving. Wordsworth Editions, Hertfordshire,
     England. 1999. p. 141.
140 Rommel, The Desert Fox, by Desmond Young. Quill-William Morrow & Co., NY, NY.
     1978. p. 98-99.

Rommel had set fire to ships and buildings along the coast, suggesting just such a move. Rommel came roaring out of the smoke and pushed the British back to Gazala.[141] Several days earlier he had received supplies and tanks as a New Year's gift from Hitler.[142] Rommel re-conquered land he had lost, up to the edge of Tobruk, and he did it in only eight days.[143] Rommel was promoted to Colonel-General and received the award, swords on oak leaves, for his Knight's Cross, the only German officer to ever win the honor.[144] The German press hailed him as a "rough-tongued, warmhearted, obviously sincere and direct soldier of genius, a man who was renowned for his ability to talk to the common soldier as one of themselves, who clearly disliked snobbery and pretension, who never dissimulated but spoke from the heart."[145] Rommel, despite the tiny number of German soldiers under his command, became a popular public figure.[146] He was viewed with contempt by the senior officers of the old school. Rommel represented the new officer of National Socialistic Germany.[147] His fame was not confined to the Axis.[148] British General Auchinleck sent a memo to

141 *Rommel - The Trail of the Fox, by David Irving. Wordsworth Editions, Hertfordshire, England. 1999. p. 144-145.*
142 *Ibid., p. 142.*
143 *Knight's Cross. David Fraser, Harper-Collins, NY, NY. 1995. p. 303.*
144 *Ibid., p. 301.*
145 *Ibid., p. 308.*
146 *Ibid., p. 309.*
147 *Ibid., p. 308.*
148 *Author's NoteThe Axis were Germany, Italy, and Australia, the forces opposing the Allies. The New American Webster Handy College Dictionary, Albert & Loy Morehead, Editor. Penguin Books, NY, NY. 1995. p. 57.*

the soldiers of the 8th Army which stated: "You will dispel all ideas that Rommel is something more than the ordinary General."[149]

149 *Ibid., p. 309.*

FIELD MARSHAL

During the spring 1942, Rommel's counter-offense leads to the re-conquest of the Cyrenaican Peninsula. The demand for additional formations and supplies was denied. Rommel blamed the German High Command who continued to prioritize the Russian Front.[150] In March 1942, the Luftwaffe gained control of the Mediterranean airspace, then supplies began to increase into North Africa.[151] The Luftwaffe sent 1,700 paratroopers, veterans of the Crete invasion and armed to the teeth with modern weapons that the Afrika Korps had not previously seen.[152] Nevertheless, the British were still being reinforced more rapidly than the Germans. Their material was being shipped to Egypt around the Cape of Africa.[153] But the British were not allowed a chance to exploit their advantage. Rommel decided to strike first.[154] With only 560 tanks against the British count of 900. [155] Rommel starts his advance on the Gazala Line. It is May 26, all day long, his tanks have been assembling, clattering and raising an enormous cloud of dust. When the attack starts, there is no one there, except truck-mounted dust-making propellers, slowly circling the desert. Rommel has slipped away undetected hours earlier on

---

150 The Rommel Papers, B.H. Liddell-Hart, Editor. Da Capo Press, NY, NY. 1953. p. 191.
151 Ibid., pp. 192-193.
152 Rommel - The Trail of the Fox, by David Irving. Wordsworth Editions, Hertfordshire, England. 1999. p. 148.
153 The Rommel Papers, B.H. Liddell-Hart, Editor. Da Capo Press, NY, NY. 1953. pp. 192-193.
154 Ibid., p. 194.
155 Ibid., p. 196.

a daring run around the British desert flank. [156] But, Rommel's Italian combat troops have failed to advance, thus enabling British to move their reserve force against Rommel, entrapping him on both sides. By the end of the first day, he has lost one-third of his tanks. In the chaos of the first day, the Luftwaffe couldn't help because they didn't know where the enemy's front lines were. Rommel pulls back, to allow identification of the enemy's positions. Now Luftwaffe Commander Waldau sends 326 planes to sweep the battlefield. The result is that Rommel wins the first phase of the battle. [157] The second phase of the battle began just as bad as the first phase. Earlier two of Rommel's top staff officers, Cause and Westphal, were wounded and captured. This left a big void in the command. Rommel's tanks were stopped by a mine field. His headquarters came under artillery fire, killing three men. He lost eleven tanks before he realized that the intelligence maps were wrong. Then, as luck would have it, Field Marshall Kesselring stopped in to see Rommel. Kesselring admired Rommel and only wanted to help. He voluntarily placed himself under Rommel and temporarily took the captured General Cause's place as Commander of all field forces west of the Gazala Line. After reviewing the battle plans together, the attack was renewed. Rommel joined the main assault force, running from platoon to platoon shouting orders. After a fierce fight, Rommel

156   Rommel - The Trail of the Fox, by David Irving. Wordsworth Editions, Hertfordshire, England. 1999. p. 157.
157   Ibid., pp. 158-159.

told a Panzer Commander near him, "I think they had enough, wave white flags at them, they'll surrender." The Panzer crewmen began to wave handkerchiefs, then the miracle happened, 3,000 enemy soldiers crawled out of their fox holes, and marched into captivity. Rommel's fingerspitzengefuhl paid off one more time. Rommel now had an established bridgehead.[158] But, his western supply line was being hampered by the British stronghold at Bir Hacheim.[159] After Rommel's summons to surrender had been rejected, he attacked.[160] It took a week of artillery bombardment and Luftwaffe dive bombings before the hungry and thirsty Free French defenders were ready to capitulate. Then the British Commanders ordered them to abandon the fort.[161] Now the third phase of the battle was ready to be carried out. Rommel has only 230 tanks remaining (he had started with 560).[162] Most of the tank losses were caused by American-built Grant tank, which the Americans had supplied to the British.[163] Rommel's attack on Gazala began June 11, 1942. First he set up a screen of anti-tank guns, which were mainly Flak 88's. The British decoyed into thinking they could reach the German tanks were gunned down by the screen. The bulk of Rommel's tanks who were waiting behind the screen then fell upon the remainder

158 Ibid., 00. 160-161.
159 Knight's Cross. David Fraser, Harper-Collins, NY, NY. 1995. p. 321.
160 The Rommel Papers, B.H. Liddell-Hart, Editor. Da Capo Press, NY, NY. 1953. p. 213.
161 Rommel, The Desert Fox, by Desmond Young. Quill-William Morrow & Co., NY, NY. 1978. p. 105.
162 Knight's Cross. David Fraser, Harper-Collins, NY, NY. 1995. p. 331.
163 Rommel - The Trail of the Fox, by David Irving. Wordsworth Editions, Hertfordshire, England. 1999. p. 157.

The 88mm Flak 36

Barrel Size: 8.8cm
Barrel Length: 21 ft.
Range: 16,000 yd.
Rate of Fire: 20 rounds per min
Weight with Tow Carriage: 12 Ton

Originally designed as a anti-aircraft gun. When it was found to have enough muzzle velocity to penetrate armour it was quickly adapted as an anti-tank gun.

of the British.[164] Rommel attacked Tobruk on June 17 by opening up a passage through the surrounding mine field. This was done by his Luftwaffe dive bombers, the Stuka. Within minutes, Rommel's tanks were inside the Fort. There was a large column of black smoke rising above Tobruk. Just before capitulation, the British had set ablaze their petrol and supply stores. Nevertheless there was enough remaining to enable Rommel to resupply his troops and feed them before continuing on to Egypt[165] As usual Rommel insisted on receiving the same rations as his troops. [166] One thousand destroyed or captured tanks and armored vehicles were taken, 400 artillery guns, and 45,000 prisoners. "For this superb achievement, I congratulate all officers and men of the Afrika Korps." Signed Rommel. Dated June 21, 1942. The next day Rommel received a wireless from Hitler's Headquarters. He had been made a Field Marshal.[167]

164 Rommel, The Desert Fox, by Desmond Young. Quill-William Morrow & Co., NY, NY. 1978. p. 106
165 Ibid., p. 107.
166 Ibid., p. 111
167 The Rommel Papers, B.H. Liddell-Hart, Editor. Da Capo Press, NY, NY. 1953. p. 232.

LACK OF SUPPLIES

Rommel had always felt that "Plan Orient" was brilliant.[168] So immediately after the fall of Tobruk, he pushed on toward Egypt. Five days later, he caught up with the New Zealand Division.[169] They were fearless and when challenged, instantly willing to fight. Rommel attacked and lost heavily, but continued on. He reached the El Almein line on June 30. He had just twelve tanks left.[170] Field Marshal Rommel's Army had finished five weeks of battle against superior British forces. The engagement had left his army at a point of exhaustion. Rommel's supply authorities had supplied him very little.[171] He had received only 5,400 replacement troops, one-third of them being the elite 1st Paratrooper Brigade under General Ramcke.[172] The British, however, were sparing no effort in replenishing the 8th Army.[173] Churchill was fighting for his political life, so to get the opposition off his back he blamed the 8th Army Generals for lack of leadership and Rommel's brilliant battlefield maneuvers as the reason's for the British misfortunes.[174] He replaces the head of the 8th Army with a new General. Then gives

168 Knight's Cross. David Fraser, Harper-Collins, NY, NY. 1995. p. 342.
169 The New Zealander Division was made up of a large number of Maoris. A Maori friend of mine told me that Rommel had said. If he had a unit of Maoris, he could conquer North Africa in a week. Author's personal communication with Marei Kingi.
170 Rommel, The Desert Fox, by Desmond Young. Quill-William Morrow & Co., NY, NY. 1978. p. 109.
171 The Rommel Papers, B.H. Liddell-Hart, Editor. Da Capo Press, NY, NY. 1953. p. 243.
172 Rommel - The Trail of the Fox, by David Irving. Wordsworth Editions, Hertfordshire, England. 1999. p. 185.
173 The Rommel Papers, B.H. Liddell-Hart, Editor. Da Capo Press, NY, NY. 1953. p. 244.
174 Rommel - The Trail of the Fox, by David Irving. Wordsworth Editions, Hertfordshire, England. 1999. pp. 176-177.

that General two extra divisions and a mass of American-made tanks and guns.[175] Churchill recognizes that the next battle in North Africa will have a major effect on the war.[176] Rommel also realizes this and decides he needs to destroy the British force before their reinforcements enable them to become too large for him to handle.[177] Rommel's plan for attack on El Alamain was August 30. He had only 203 German Panzers[178] and 85 percent of his support vehicles consisted of captured enemy machines.[179] But, the British General Montgomery had 767 tanks and several hundred six-pounder anti-tank guns. Rommel took a desperate gamble with this attack,[180] because not only was he short on equipment, but his main weakness was that his Panzers had barely enough fuel for 100 miles.[181] Rommel was extremely sick at the time of his scheduled launch and confided to his doctor that he may not attack. At 10:00 p.m., Rommel gives the go ahead. Almost at once his tanks advanced into a minefield. No one thought much of it because they had been in minefields before, but before they could finish clearing the mines, parachute flares illuminated the whole battlefield. Then, a non-stop air attack began.[182]

175 Rommel, The Desert Fox, by Desmond Young. Quill-William Morrow & Co., NY, NY. 1978. p. 142.
176 The Rommel Papers, B.H. Liddell-Hart, Editor. Da Capo Press, NY, NY. 1953. p. 244.
177 Ibid., p. 245.
178 Rommel - The Trail of the Fox, by David Irving. Wordsworth Editions, Hertfordshire, England. 1999. p. 189.
179 The Rommel Papers, B.H. Liddell-Hart, Editor. Da Capo Press, NY, NY. 1953. p. 245.
180 Rommel - The Trail of the Fox, by David Irving. Wordsworth Editions, Hertfordshire, England. 1999. p. 191.
181 Ibid., p. 189.
182 Ibid., pp. 190-191.

Rommel's Fingerspitzengefuhl came to him. It told him to "stop the attack." Afrika Korps Commander Bayerlein went to Rommel's truck. There he found Rommel being attended to by his doctor, lying sick and helpless. Rommel told him to break off the battle. Bayerlein said this is only the first morning. "Let's give the battle a chance to continue."[183] So Rommel agreed to advance around the enemy's main position by moving east past the Alamel Halfa Ridge, turn north, and wheel in behind them. But due to lack of petrol, he cut his move east short and moved toward the ridge only to find the British massed behind it. A short time later, at dusk, the bombers came and for the rest of the day and into the night, the Royal Air Force continued their attack. Rommel's troops took heavy losses, his gamble had failed.[184] The following morning, Rommel withdrew, Montgomery, a very cautious man, failed to cut off Rommel's evacuation, no doubt due to Rommel's reputation.[185] The final casualty list showed the Afrika Korps having 2,940 dead, wounded, missing and the British having 1,640 dead, wounded, missing. On the material side, the Africa Corps had lost 50 tanks, 35 anti-tank guns, and 15 field guns. The British lost 68 tanks, 18 anti-tank guns, no field guns.[186] A few days after the battle, Rommel received sick leave and flew to Germany for treatment.[187]

183 *Rommel, The Desert Fox, by Desmond Young. Quill-William Morrow & Co., NY, NY. 1978. pp. 146-147.*
184 *Rommel - The Trail of the Fox, by David Irving. Wordsworth Editions, Hertfordshire, England. 1999. pp. 192-193.*
185 *The Rommel Papers, B.H. Liddell-Hart, Editor. Da Capo Press, NY, NY. 1953. p. 280.*
186 *Ibid., 283.*
187 *Rommel, The Desert Fox, by Desmond Young, Quill-William Morrow & Co., NY, NY. 1978. p.147.*

THE BRITISH STRIKE BACK

Field Marshal Rommel had severe stomach problems, his blood pressure gave him trouble, and number of other ailments derived from the stomach problem. It was recommended he be on leave for six weeks. He knew that if the Afrika Korps were to stay in Egypt, the next battle would be against an enormously well outfitted British force. [188] Rommel returned to Germany a triumphant hero. He was given a ceremonial baton. But before he returned to his home in Wiener Neustadt, Austria.[189] Hitler had something to show him. It was a prototype of the Tiger tank and a multiple mortar weapon. Then Hitler told him of a secret bomb Germany was developing that could knock a man down two miles away. Rommel later began to have doubts about what Hitler had told him and said to his wife: "I wonder if Hitler told me about those weapons to keep me quiet." Rommel had for the first time questioned Hitler's motives.[190] Rommel told Hitler of the Afrika Korps problems. Number one was lack of supplies, in particular petrol; number two was enemy air superiority; and number three, the Italians were useless except for defense. [191] Hitler told Rommel: "Don't worry, I am

188 Knight's Cross, by David Fraser, Harper Collins, NY, NY. 1955. pp. 362-363.
189 Ibid., 364-365.
190 Rommel, The Desert Fox, by Desmond Young, Quill-William Morrow & Co., NY, NY. 1978. p.148.
191 Rommel, The Trail of the Fox, by David Irving, Wordsworth Editions, Hertfordshire, England. 1999. p. 198.
192 Rommel, The Desert Fox, by Desmond Young, Quill-William Morrow & Co., NY, NY. 1978. p.147.

Montgomery's Army had grown to 1,029 tanks and almost one-quarter million men.[193]

Rommel had been home only three weeks when a phone call came for him at the hospital where he was a patient. It was Hitler, he told Rommel the British were on the offensive and his replacement General Stumme was missing in action. Hitler asked him if he felt good enough to return to Africa. Although still a very sick man, Rommel agreed to return to his beloved Afrika Korps.[194] The British had attacked on October 23, 1942. The Battle of Alamein had begun.[195] When the British attacked, of the 1,029 tanks they had, 500 were armed with a 75mm gun. The Afrika Korps had only 38 tanks with 75 mm guns. Of the 210 Panzers they possessed, only 30 were Panzer IV's, the rest were either out of date or decrepit.[196] On his way back to Africa, Rommel was told that the Afrika Korps had only three days of fuel left.[197] When he arrived on the 25th, the battle was already hopeless. "Rommel could do nothing," stated General Bayerlein.[198] But, after five days, the British still could not break through the German lines. Rommel's tiny and insufficiently supplied army was holding. The British had lost 10,000 men, but were

193 Rommel, The Trail of the Fox, by David Irving, Wordsworth Editions, Hertfordshire, England. 1999. p. 201.
194 Rommel, The Desert Fox, by Desmond Young, Quill-William Morrow & Co., NY, NY. 1978. p.149.
195 Knight's Cross, by David Fraser, Harper Collins, NY, NY. 1955. p. 368.
196 The Rommel Papers, B.H. Liddell-Hart, Editor. Da Capo Press, NY, NY. 1953. pp. 296-297.
197 Rommel, The Trail of the Fox, by David Irving, Wordsworth Editions, Hertfordshire, England. 1999. p. 200.
198 Rommel, The Desert Fox, by Desmond Young, Quill-William Morrow & Co., NY, NY. 1978. p.149.

were able to replace them.[199] Rommel knew that due to the enemy air superiority, it would only be a matter of time before a breakthrough would occur.[200] The battle had become a "material schlact," the one with the most material wins.[201] Then on October 28, Rommel receives an order to execute all captured commandos. Rommel burns the order in full view of his subordinates.[202] Rommel had given the order that the Afrika Korps would not abuse any prisoners.[203]

On the night of November 1, relays of British night bombers began to attack the southern end of the German defensive line. Simultaneously hundreds of guns started shelling the same area.[204] Then a mass of infantry broke through on a 4,000 yard wide front which opened a passage for British armor. Rommel had an anti-tank gun screen waiting and gunned down 87 tanks.[205] But the enemy kept pouring a steady flow of reinforcements into the passage.[206] Rommel knew that this was the end. Now it was his duty to save what was left of the Afrika Korps.[207]

199 Rommel, The Trail of the Fox, by David Irving, Wordsworth Editions, Hertfordshire, England. 1999. p. 205.
200 The Rommel Papers, B.H. Liddell-Hart, Editor. Da Capo Press, NY, NY. 1953. p. 300.
201 Knight's Cross, by David Fraser, Harper Collins, NY, NY. 1955. p. 369.
202 Ibid., 376.
203 Rommel, The Desert Fox, Desmond Young, Quill-William Morrow & Co., NY, NY. 1978. P.127-128
204 The Rommel Papers, B.H. Liddell-Hart, Editor. Da Capo Press, NY, NY. 1953. p. 317.
205 Rommel, The Desert Fox, by Desmond Young, Quill-William Morrow & Co., NY, NY. 1978. p.151.
206 The Rommel Papers, B.H. Liddell-Hart, Editor. Da Capo Press, NY, NY. 1953. p. 317.
207 Knight's Cross, by David Fraser, Harper Collins, NY, NY. 1955. p. 380.

THE MAGNIFICENT ESCAPE

Concealed from his superiors, Rommel developed an escape plan he called the "Fuka Plan." Fuka is a village on the Mediterranean, 60 miles west of El Alamein. It is from here that he began his escape. The road is well protected from flanking maneuvers. An escape timetable has been worked out and provisional points allocated on the map.[208] Rommel takes count of his remaining tanks. He will need them to cover his escape. He learns that he has only 30 tanks and a couple days of fuel.[209] Rommel warns his combat units, like the elite Ramcke Paratrooper Brigade, who had fought so well for him, that there may not be enough motor transport to carry them.[210] He orders his lead elements to move to the Fuka line. It is late on November 2.[211] The next day, Rommel receives an order from Hitler. It read: "The El Almein position will be held to the last man. There is to be no retreat. It will be victory or death." Signed Adolf Hitler.[212] Field Marshal Rommel cannot make up his mind whether to carry out the order or not. That night Rommel goes out into the desert alone to ponder the order. The next morning, he orders a full withdrawal of the Afrika Korps. Rommel has disobeyed Hitler.[213]

208 Rommel, The Trail of the Fox, by David Irving, Wordsworth Editions, Hertfordshire, England. 1999. pp. 206-207.
209 Knight's Cross, by David Fraser, Harper Collins, NY, NY. 1955. p. 380.
210 Rommel, The Trail of the Fox, by David Irving, Wordsworth Editions, Hertfordshire, England. 1999. p. 207.
211 Knight's Cross, by David Fraser, Harper Collins, NY, NY. 1955. p. 380.
212 Rommel, The Desert Fox, by Desmond Young, Quill-William Morrow & Co., NY, NY. 1978. p.152.
213 Knight's Cross, by David Fraser, Harper Collins, NY, NY. 1955. pp. 382-383.

The column leaving Fuka is 60 miles long. It has tanks, guns, personnel-carriers, trucks and cars. They carry 70,000 German and Italian troops.[214] As luck would have it, just as Rommel had embarked, a shipment of 1,200 tons of petrol had arrived. All the way west, Rommel made the skillful use of mines, road demolitions, and booby-traps to slow the British. [216] Montgomery tried to out-flank Rommel, by turning right and racing to the coastal road, each time the British did they had encircled nothing. On November 6, Montgomery closed his main trap, his 4th attempt. But the Desert Fox had again escaped.[217] Rommel's loyal veterans fought desperate rearguard actions, even though they had no food or water.[218] "The only cheering event was the unexpected reappearance of General Ramcke at Rommel's bus on November 7. Ramcke swung him a snappy salute and tartly announced that he and 800 of his Luftwaffe paratroopers, written off by Rommel on November 4, had ambushed a British truck convoy, stolen its trucks, and driven through the enemy army to rejoin Rommel's force. There was a malicious delight in Ramcke's metallic smile" (Ramcke's teeth were made of metal).[219] Six hundred miles short of Tripoli, Rommel ran out of

214 Rommel, The Trail of the Fox, by David Irving, Wordsworth Editions, Hertfordshire, England. 1999. p. 216.
215 Ibid., p. 207.
216 Rommel, The Desert Fox, by Desmond Young, Quill-William Morrow & Co., NY, NY. 1978. p.154.
217 Rommel, The Trail of the Fox, by David Irving, Wordsworth Editions, Hertfordshire, England. 1999. p. 217.
218 Ibid., p.216.
219 Ibid., 218.

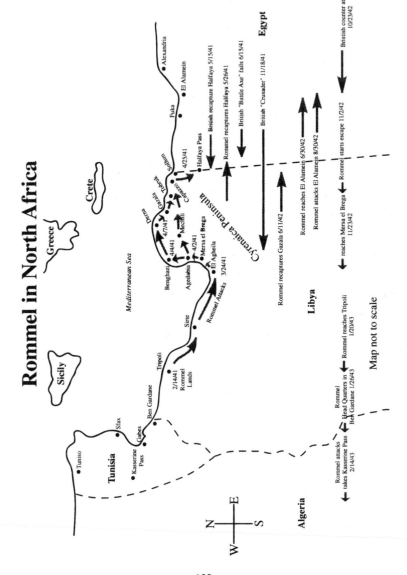

Rommel in North Africa

Map not to scale

gas. Just then a rain storm hit. The desert turned to gumbo and the British became bogged down. Rommel's luck had come through again. The Luftwaffe managed to airlift 80 tons of petrol to Rommel. He filled up and escaped again.[220] Rommel had retraced his steps back halfway across the Cyrenaican Peninsula when he ran out of fuel again. On the morning of November 21, thousands of supply crates and oil drums were sighted along the Mediterranean coastline on his right. It was the cargo of a torpedoed supply ship. With this fuel the Desert Fox safely escaped again. Rommel jotted down in his notebook, "Miracles do happen." By November 23, he had completed the trip across the Cyrenaican. He had traveled 800 miles from El Alamein, virtually without a loss.[221] At Mersa el Brega on the western edge of the Cyrenaican, Hitler ordered Rommel to stop and put up a defense against the British. Rommel disagreed.[222] (Rommel was on talking terms with Hitler again because Hitler had rescinded his "victory or death" order and approved of Rommel's decision to withdraw.) Rommel decided to visit the Fuhrer personally. He arrived at Hitler's headquarters on November 28. There Rommel experienced, for the first time, one of Hitler's notorious rages.[223] Rommel had told Hitler that to fight in North Africa was hopeless and that it would be better to save the Afrika Korps, so they could fight again later. Hitler became furious, scream-

220 Ibid., 222.
221 Ibid., 222.
222 Ibid., p. 222.
223 Knight's Cross, by David Fraser, Harper Collins, NY, NY. 1955. pp. 392-393.

would be better to save the Afrika Korps, so they could fight again later. Hitler became furious, screaming. He called Rommel a defeatist and his men cowards. Rommel answered back, "Come to Africa and see for yourself." "Get out of her," screamed Hitler. "I have more important things to think about." Rommel saluted and left. A few seconds later, Hitler apologized and told Rommel to come back tomorrow and we'll discuss it. The next day, Hitler asked the Luftwaffe head, Goering, to speak to Mussolini about supplies on Rommel's behalf.[224] In the meantime, Rommel had modified his plan. Now the Afrika Korps would move to Tunisia, join with General Nehring's force (having just arrived in Africa) and "surprise" attack the inexperienced Americans (the Americans had just landed in northwest Africa).[225] Mussolini partly agreed with Rommel's plan because he appreciated Rommel's efforts in saving his army. Mussolini said to Rommel, "Your escape from El Alamein has been a masterpiece."[226] Rommel immediately began moving his Afrika Korps toward Tripoli. A few days later, Montgomery was sighted on the outflanking move around Rommel, just as Rommel had predicted. But when daylight came the following day, the Mersa el Grega line was empty. The Desert Fox had vanished again.[227]

224 Rommel, The Desert Fox, by Desmond Young, Quill-William Morrow & Co., NY, NY. 1978.
     p.154-155.
225 Rommel, The Trail of the Fox, by David Irving, Wordsworth Editions, Hertfordshire,
     England. 1999. p. 226.
226 Ibid., 216.
227 Ibid., 228.

KASSERINE PASS

On January 26, Rommel set up his headquarters in Ben Gardane, Tunisia. He had traveled almost 2,000 miles the past two and one-half months on virtually no supplies, and his convoy had constantly been attacked by the Royal Air Force. Rommel's health was at a new low. He had headaches, insomnia, and frequent fainting spells, and still would not take sick leave. His poor health did not go unnoticed by the Axis powers. They formed the First Army which subsumed Rommel's command.[228] Just then he reached Tunisia and was astonished at the amount of material the Italians were able to ship to Africa. It was as though Rome suddenly realized the danger they were in. But Rommel understood that the Allies were receiving many times over what the Axis was receiving.[229] The new First Army was actually the old German-Italian Panzer Army under a new name. The new head was General von Arnim.[230] Rommel was promoted to head all Axis Forces in Tunisia.[231] But Rommel didn't see it that way and refuses to cooperate with von Arnim. On February 2, 1943, the German 6th Army surrenders at Stalingrad, Russia.[232] A few days later, Rommel agrees to cooperate with von Arnim for the good of

228 *Knight's Cross, by David Fraser, Harper Collins, NY, NY. 1955. p. 397.*
229 *The Rommel Papers, B.H. Liddell-Hart, Editor. Da Capo Press, NY, NY. 1953. p. 358.*
230 *Rommel, The Desert Fox, by Desmond Young, Quill-William Morrow & Co., NY, NY. 1978. pp.156-157.*
231 *Ibid., p. 157.*
232 *Knight's Cross, by David Fraser, Harper Collins, NY, NY. 1955. p. 566.*

the "Fatherland." In the meantime, American General Eisenhower's planned to attack Rommel's lifeline.[233] Rommel responded by selecting a vulnerable place to strike the Americans first. The American 2nd Corps occupied a plain between Gafsa and Fondouk. Directly behind the 2nd Corps was the Kasserine Pass. Sixty miles to the southeast lay the Mediterranean. With his 21st Panzer Division now replenished, Rommel fell upon the Americans. The 2nd Corps' forward positions were quickly overrun. Rommel continued on and took Kasserine Pass. A large salient had been established in the allied lines.[234] Rommel had got what he wanted; to show that he was not a defeatist[235] and that the Afrika Korps, despite their 2,000 mile odyssey, could still fight and win.[236] Rommel fought one more battle in Africa, but was too sick to bring a climax to his plan. On March 9, 1943, Rommel starts for home. After arrival, he is awarded diamonds for his Knight's Cross. Rommel is the first German officer to receive such an honor.[237]

233 Rommel, The Trail of the Fox, by David Irving, Wordsworth Editions, Hertfordshire, England. 1999. pp. 242-243.
234 Rommel, The Desert Fox, by Desmond Young, Quill-William Morrow & Co., NY, NY. 1978. pp. 157-158.
235 Ibid. p.159.
236 Rommel, The Trail of the Fox, by David Irving, Wordsworth Editions, Hertfordshire, England. 1999. p. 243.
237 Ibid., pp.256-257.

The Battle of Kasserine Pass

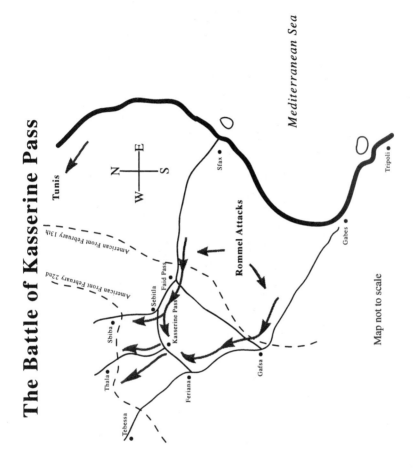

Map not to scale

HONEST ASSESSMENT

Nine weeks had gone by since Rommel had returned home for treatment. He has spent the time writing his memoirs of the two years spent in Africa. Rommel now becomes anxious for a new command. Finally, on May 8, he is ordered to Berlin for further orders. [238] The previous day, General von Arnim had surrendered in North Africa. Two hundred thirty-eight thousand soldiers passed with him into Allied captivity [239] Hitler visited with Rommel about the Mediterranean situation, then said: "I should have listened to you." [240] Rommel was then posted to the Fuhrer's headquarters as a military advisor.[241] For the next few months, Rommel attended daily situation conferences which were held either at Berlin, Rastenburg (Prussia) or Berchtesgaden (Bavaria). He heard news from all fronts. [242] Rommel privately presented Hitler with an honest assessment of the war and challenged him about the future of the German people. Hitler said he knew there was little chance of winning the war, then stated, "no one will make peace with me."[243] Rommel now realized that Hitler was willing to drag his whole nation down with him.

238   Ibid., pp. 261-262.
239   Knight's Cross, by David Fraser, Harper Collins, NY, NY. 1955. p. 414.
240   Ibid., 432.
241   Rommel, The Desert Fox, by Desmond Young, Quill-William Morrow & Co., NY, NY. 1978. p.164.
242   Knight's Cross, by David Fraser, Harper Collins, NY, NY. 1955. p. 432.
243   Rommel, The Trail of the Fox, by David Irving, Wordsworth Editions, Hertfordshire, England. 1999. p. 265.

Rommel, who had grown up under the old Prussian tradition of unconditional obedience, now began to recognize that there are limits to obedience.[244] On July 4, 1943, Hitler begins "Operation Citadel," his Russian counter-offensive. Six days later, the British-American force, code-named "Operation Husky" under Eisenhower invades Sicily.[245] Rommel has a private war conference with Hitler, then on July 15, Hitler appoints Rommel as Commander of Army Group B, with orders to organize resistance against Italy. Rommel develops a two-phase plan. Phase I was a gradual move into Italy with the assignment of helping the Italians. Phase II was to be taken only if the Italians defected. The assignment would be to disarm the Italians and take possession of their equipment, and if needed, subdue them as enemies.[246] Phase I begins immediately. Then on July 26, Mussolini is voted out of office and arrested.[247] Hitler has his Luftwaffe Airborne Commandos rescue Mussolini from his captors. It is a brilliant paratrooper operation and Mussolini is moved to Lake Garda with a SS[248] guard.[249] In Russia citadel is faltering, Hitler decides to cancel the Russian offensive and also pull out of Sicily. It is August 4, 12 days later the German withdrawal from Sicily is complete, and the remainder of the

244   The Rommel Papers, B.H. Liddell-Hart, Editor. Da Capo Press, NY, NY. 1953. p. 428.
245   Knight's Cross, by David Fraser, Harper Collins, NY, NY. 1955. p. 566.
246   Ibid., 437.
247   Ibid., 441.
248   The SS was originally established as a protection squad for the Nazi party elite, later under Heinrich Himmler, it evolved into having a completely different ideology. Knight's Cross, by David Fraser, Harper Collins, NY, NY. 1955. p. 102.
249   Ibid., p. 450.

70,000 soldiers are safely in Italy. Hitler's plan was to keep the Allies out of German by using Italy as a base.[250] An Armistice between Italy and the Allies was signed on September 8, 1943. Rommel immediately begins Phase II of the Italian takeover. Rommel's troops arrest 82 Generals, 13,000 officers, and 402,600 soldiers of the Italian Army.[251] One day after the Armistice is signed with Italy, the Allies landing craft unload on the beaches in Salerno, Italy. General Eisenhower is now the Allies top commander.[252] It was during this period that Rommel experienced the SS's atrocious behavior firsthand. He had heard about SS actions in Poland, but didn't really believe it. Now it was happening in his theater of command. Rommel was indignant because he was not allowed to discipline the SS, but he had the freedom to control the location of his troops, so he ordered the SS out of Milan.[253] Meanwhile the Allies advanced inland from the Salerno beachhead.[254] Hitler decided to join the southern Italy command which was under General Kesserling, with the Northern Italy command, under Rommel. He was about to give the combined command to Rommel.[255] When Hitler's Chief of Army Personnel, General Schmunt, told him that because of Rommel's resentment toward Italy for not supplying

250 Ibid., pp. 438-443.
251 Ibid., pp. 445-446.
252 The Rommel Papers, B.H. Liddell-Hart, Editor. Da Capo Press, NY, NY. 1953. p. 444.
253 Rommel, The Desert Fox, by Desmond Young, Quill-William Morrow & Co., NY, NY. 1978. p.166.
254 Rommel, The Trail of the Fox, by David Irving, Wordsworth Editions, Hertfordshire, England. 1999. p. 278.
255 Ibid., p. 280.

his Army in North Africa, it would better for Rommel to have nothing to do with Italy,[256] so Hitler moves Rommel and Army Group B headquarters to France. On the way to France Rommel stops at his new home in Herrlingen near Ulm.[257] During the past few months, the Allies had been bombing German cities which were of strategic interest to the war effort. Rommel's home in Wiener-Neustadt, Austria, was close to the Messerschmitt airplane factory and he feared for his family's safety. So he had them move to Herrlingen, Germany.[258] Rommel's headquarters was moved to La Roche-Guyon; a grand old castle northwest of Paris, the castle was full of historical intrigue which aroused no interest in Rommel. Unfortunately Rommel had two superiors. He took instructions directly from Hitler and was also subordinate to Field Marshal von Rundstedt.[259] von Rundstedt at 68 was Germany's most senior officer.[260] He was an aristocratic dignified officer of the old Prussian school and a very capable orthodox strategist.[261] Rommel's new assignment was to inspect all defenses on the coastline facing England. He outlined how a six mile wide impregnable swath of minefield and bunkers was to be built along the

256 Ibid., p. 283.
257 Ibid. p. 285.
258 Ibid., p. 275.
259 Rommel, The Desert Fox, by Desmond Young, Quill-William Morrow & Co., NY, NY. 1978. pp.169-170.
260 Rommel, The Trail of the Fox, by David Irving, Wordsworth Editions, Hertfordshire, England. 1999. p. 286.
261 Rommel, The Desert Fox, by Desmond Young, Quill-William Morrow & Co., NY, NY. 1978. p.170.
262 Rommel, The Trail of the Fox, by David Irving, Wordsworth Editions, Hertfordshire, England. 1999. p. 285.

"Atlantic Wall."[262] Rommel got up very early, traveled fast, visited sites very quickly, and had a "fingerspitzengefuhl" in locating where something was wrong.[263] Rommel had accepted his new assignment with his usual vigor and promptitude.[264] He repeated constantly," We must stop the enemy in the water." To make a landing difficult, he devised many gadgets, such as beams, poles, and blocks, some with mines, all driven into the beaches at low-water mark. He prepared concrete bunkers, along with dummy batteries, dummy minefields and dummy emplacements. To impede aircraft landings, he drove poles into any open field, and was prepared to flood rear areas to handicap paratroop landings. It was now early January 1944, Rommel felt the invasion was imminent, so there was an urgency to complete his "Atlantic Wall." There was 3,000 miles of coast and with only 59 divisions to defend it, Rommel proposed keeping the armor in the rear until point of attack was identified, then at the right moment launch a counteroffensive.[265] von Rundstedt and Rommel got along with each other, but Rommel realized he needed to be independent, so he could move at a moment's notice. Rommel presented this concept to his superiors and on January 1, 1943 was promoted to Commander in Chief of the German Armies from the Loire River, in Southern France,

263 Rommel, The Desert Fox, by Desmond Young, Quill-William Morrow & Co., NY, NY. 1978. p.169.
264 Knight's Cross, by David Fraser, Harper Collins, NY, NY. 1955. p. 454.
265 Rommel, The Desert Fox, by Desmond Young, Quill-William Morrow & Co., NY, NY. 1978. pp.174-177.

North to the Netherlands.[266] Later that same month, the Allies landed at Anzio, a short distance south of Rome, the exact location where Rommel had predicted they would come ashore. The German high command's Panzer reserves were in Central France. There they would remain as "reserves" for both the southern front, as well as the impending invasion of the east. Rommel's plan to use the "Reserves" as part of his western coastal defense system just went out the window.[267] Rommel then began an inspection of the Normandy coastline and found them to be inadequate.[268] A month later in early March, Rommel wrote to his wife and stated he needed more time to reinforce the defenses.[269] Rommel spent the next weeks hunting and walking in the woods around his headquarters at the beautiful La Roche Guyon. The hosts of the chateau were the Rochefoucauld family. In this part of France, the upper classes feared the consequences of communism in Europe.[270] This made them and the populace largely pro-German. The German intelligence reported the invasion would begin during the first three weeks of May.[271] Rommel's "Fingerspitzengefuhl" again went to work and he predicted the Allies would land on the beaches of Normandy. Again Rommel tried to move the Panzer

266   Ibid., 170.
267   Rommel, The Trail of the Fox, by David Irving, Wordsworth Editions, Hertfordshire, England. 1999. p. 296.
268   Ibid., p.297.
269   Ibid., p.305.
270   Hitler had come into power on an anti-communist platform. Knight's Cross, by David Fraser, Harper Collins, NY, NY. 1955. p. 106.
271   Ibid., p. 317, pp. 314-315.

reserves closer to Normandy. Again General von Rundstedt refused based on his orthodox view that the invasion would be in the north at Pas de Calais.[272] Next Rommel's Chief of Staff, General Cause, had received his own command. Rommel was offered two replacements for the position, naturally Rommel picked the Swabian applicant. His name is Hans Speidel. General Speidel had just won the Knight's Cross in Russia. Little did Rommel know, that Speidel had been "planted" in Rommel's headquarters by anti-Hitler members of the General's staff. Speidel's assignment was to win Rommel over to their cause.[273] Rommel felt comfortable with General Speidel in charge, so he signed out on leave and went to Germany to attend his wife's birthday. Lucy's birthday was June 6. At 6:15 that morning the phone rang. It was Speidel, he told Rommel the invasion has started.[274]

272 Rommel, The Desert Fox, by Desmond Young, Quill-William Morrow & Co., NY, NY. 1978. p.179.
273 Rommel, The Trail of the Fox, by David Irving, Wordsworth Editions, Hertfordshire, England. 1999. pp. 309-310, p.318.
274 Knight's Cross, by David Fraser, Harper Collins, NY, NY. 1955. p. 485

BETRAYAL

The night of June 5 was dark in Normandy. In the late hours of dusk, a continuous drone of bombers began, soon exploding bombs could be heard along the Normandy coastline. Then at approximately one o'clock a.m., thousands of paratroopers dropped into the darkness. Immediately following them were hundreds of gliders, silently landing with guns, vehicles and men. The German commanders raced to report the landings, whereupon, the defense machinery went into action. Soon an inland battle had erupted. The paratroopers advanced on the coast to help establish a bridgehead in the coastal defenses. The first town to be occupied by the allies was St. Mere Eglise. Members of the American 505 Paratrooper Brigade had taken control of the village.[275] Just as dawn was breaking, all of a sudden the Allied Navy began a bombardment of the Normandy Beach defenses. This was followed by Allied airplanes converging on the Beach defenses, as well. The German soldiers who had survived this inferno began to fight back. At several places, they succeeded in holding the Allies advance on the Beach, but their line was so thinly held, that eventually the Allies broke through and linked up with the paratroopers who had dropped in during the previous night. The German divisions on the defensive quickly brought up their reserves. Those reserves

---

275 *The author served in the 505 Paratrooper Brigade from 1962-1965. I know from personal knowledge that St. Mere Eglise was the first town liberated in France.*

German Defenses During D-Day Landings, June 6th, 1944

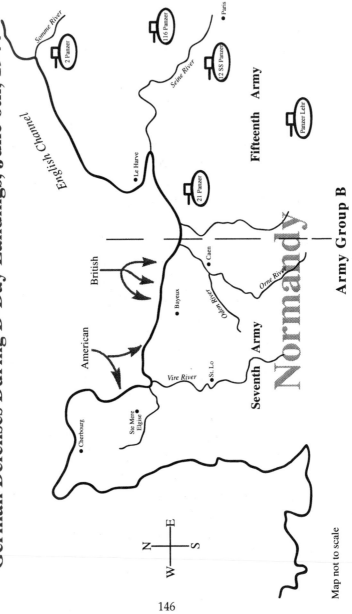

on foot were continuously attacked by dive bombers. When there were no more reserves available, the front began to crumble. On the evening of June 6, the situation looked bleak. The British had gained a large bridgehead; the Americans had established two bridgeheads. The German commanders now waited nervously for the arrival of the Panzer reserves and the Armored Force reserves. General von Rundstedt had put two Panzer Divisions on alert, but the High Command didn't believe Normandy was the main landing and wouldn't release the Panzers. By the time they were released to help, the Allies had already gained a foothold in France.[276] Rommel was right again. If von Rundestedt and the High Command had listened to him, the Allies would not have made it into France. [277] Rommel returned to France on June 7 and immediately began evaluating the battle.[278] The battlefield was in a restricted space, decisions were needed instantly. This was how Rommel worked best.[279] However, movement, including Rommel's, was next to impossible due to Allied air superiority. The German front had held up until now, but the battle had turned into a "material schlacht"[280] again. The battle was beginning to favor the Allies.[281] The American bridgehead was potentially more dangerous than the British

276 The Rommel Papers, B.H. Liddell-Hart, Editor. Da Capo Press, NY, NY. 1953. pp. 471-474.
277 Rommel, The Desert Fox, by Desmond Young, Quill-William Morrow & Co., NY, NY. 1978. p.180.
278 Knight's Cross, by David Fraser, Harper Collins, NY, NY. 1955. p. 492.
279 Ibid., 497.
280 "Material schlacht" is a German word which can be best defined as those with the most material win the war. Knight's Cross, by David Fraser, Harper Collins, NY, NY. 1955. p. 376.
281 Ibid., p. 494-495.

bridgehead. Rommel's plan to move against the Americans was vetoed by Hitler.[282] Hitler wanted to defend the port at Cherbourg, thus denying the enemy a port to bring supplies ashore.[283]

On June 17, a conference was called in France to discuss the invasion. Rommel began the conference by giving a full report on their impossible situation.[284] Hitler then gave promises of miraculous methods that would be used to stop the Allied supply line. [285] The next ten days, Rommel became more aware of a coming catastrophe, that he could do nothing to stop, but for which he felt responsible.[286] On June 18, Hitler returned to Germany because a bomb had exploded beside his headquarters.[287] On June 29, Rommel and von Rundstedt held another conference with Hitler at Berchtesgaden, hoping that Hitler would see how futile the war was and plan accordingly. Rommel tried twice to address the issue. Hitler finally told Rommel to leave the room.[288] Both Field Marshals, von Rundestedt and Rommel, expected to be relieved of their duties, but only von Rundstedt was recalled. He was replaced by Field Marshal von Kluge.[289] When von Kluge came aboard, he told Rommel flatly that he had to start taking orders like everyone else. No doubt

282   The Rommel Papers, B.H. Liddell-Hart, Editor. Da Capo Press, NY, NY. 1953. p. 478
283   Knight's Cross, by David Fraser, Harper Collins, NY, NY. 1955. p. 499.
284   The Rommel Papers, B.H. Liddell-Hart, Editor. Da Capo Press, NY, NY. 1953. p. 478.
285   Knight's Cross, by David Fraser, Harper Collins, NY, NY. 1955. p. 499.
286   Ibid., p. 501.
287   The Rommel Papers, B.H. Liddell-Hart, Editor. Da Capo Press, NY, NY. 1953. p. 479.
288   Rommel, The Trail of the Fox, by David Irving, Wordsworth Editions, Hertfordshire, England. 1999. p. 363.
289   The Rommel Papers, B.H. Liddell-Hart, Editor. Da Capo Press, NY, NY. 1953. p. 480.

in reference to Rommel's actions at the last conference with Hitler.[290] One month after D-Day, Rommel still held the British bridgehead in-check. With his supplies depleted, Rommel decided they should keep fighting to obtain peace terms that were not so severe. Montgomery ordered a massive bombardment on Rommel's troops, who occupied the medieval city of Caen.[291] For forty minutes, 80,000 shells and 2,560 tons of the Allied Air Force explosives leveled the city. But Rommel won a tactical victory when his 12th SS Panzer Division, average age 18½ years, crawled out of the rubble and with only a handful of Tiger tanks destroyed 103 British tanks, and put the enemy on the run.[292] It did not take Rommel's Commander von Kluge long before he too arrived at the same conclusion as Rommel, about the imminent catastrophe facing the German Army west. On July 16, Rommel wrote an "ultimatum" to Hitler, "The end is near, the time of truth has arrived." von Kluge endorsed it and sent it to the High Command.[293] Rommel's assistant, Speidel, knew this was the opportunity he had been waiting for, he immediately sent for Caesar von Hofacker, a Lieutenant Colonel in the Luftwaffe. Rommel met with von Hofacker for about thirty minutes. Afterwards von Hofacker told a fellow conspirator that Rommel is willing to lead the Armistice talks

290 Rommel, The Trail of the Fox, by David Irving, Wordsworth Editions, Hertfordshire, England. 1999. p. 367.

291 Caen was a mere eight miles from the British landing area on the coast of Normandy. The Rommel Papers, B.H. Liddell-Hart, Editor. Da Capo Press, NY, NY. 1953. p. 275.

292 Ibid., 369.

293 Knight's Cross, by David Fraser, Harper Collins, NY, NY. 1955. pp. 509-510.

with the Allies.[294] Over the next few days Rommel was haunted by the thought of defeat. On July 17, he drove to the front, met with his commanders and discussed strategy for the coming days.[295] On the return from the front, Rommel's car was strafed by Allied aircraft. His car veered off the road and crashed into a tree, causing Rommel to crush his skull.[296] The following day, the British attacked at precisely a point Rommel's "Fingerspitzengefuhl" told him they would. By the end of the day, the British attack had stalled. The Germans were still in control of the front line. Rommel did not lose his last battle.[297] The next day, July 18, 1944, Colonel Klaus von Stauffenberg[298] planted a suitcase bomb in Hitler's War Conference Room at Rastenburg, East Prussia. He escaped to Berlin and announced that the Gestapo had killed Hitler. That evening the German radio interrupted the news with an announcement of an assassination attempt on Hitler's life. Hitler was alive![299] By midnight the same day, von Stauffenberg was placed in front of a firing

294 *Rommel, The Trail of the Fox, by David Irving, Wordsworth Editions, Hertfordshire, England. 1999. pp. 371-373.*

295 *Ibid., 373.*

296 *Ibid., p. 381.*

297 *Knight's Cross, by David Fraser, Harper Collins, NY, NY. 1955. p. 513.*

298 *Author's Note Col. von Stauffenberg was a cousin to Col. von Hofacker. von Hofacker was adjutant to Gen. von Stulpnagel, the military Governor of France. von Stulpnagel had helped Gen. Speidel get the appointment on Rommel's staff. All were caught and executed by Hitler, except Speidel who had escaped from prison and went to the Western Allies. Hundreds were executed based on only the slightest evidence. Rommel, The Trail of the Fox, by David Irving, Wordsworth Editions, Hertfordshire, England. 1999. pp. 318, 370, 373. Knight's Cross, by David Fraser, Harper Collins, NY, NY. 1955. p. 526. Rommel, The Desert Fox, by Desmond Young, Quill-William Morrow & Co., NY, NY. 1978. p. 222.*

299 *Rommel, The Trail of the Fox, by David Irving, Wordsworth Editions, Hertfordshire, England. 1999. pp. 384-385.*

squad and executed. Within hours, the Gestapo interrogations and torture began producing a long list of conspirators.[300] In the meantime, Rommel's recovery astonished the surgeons. He was moved to a Paris hospital, then home on August 8 for more rest. The doctors told Rommel it would be two months before he could return to work.[301] On October 7, Rommel is ordered to report to Berlin for the purpose of discussing future employment. But his "fingerspitzengefuhl" tells him there is danger in going to Berlin. Rommel tells General Keitel in Berlin that he cannot travel due to advice from his doctors.[302] At 12:00 noon on October 14, two Generals, Burgdorf and Maisel, from the Personnel Department of the High Command in Berlin, arrive at Rommel's home in Herrlingen. They talked with Rommel in private for one hour, whereupon they went outside and stood in the garden. Rommel went upstairs to see his wife, when he entered the room, his wife noticed the strangest expression on his face. She immediately asked, "What has happened?" Rommel answers, "They suspect me of participating in the plot to assassinate Hitler. They presented me with Mayor Goerdeler's[303] list of people

300 Knight's Cross, by David Fraser, Harper Collins, NY, NY. 1955. p. 522-523.
301 Rommel, The Trail of the Fox, by David Irving, Wordsworth Editions, Hertfordshire, England. 1999. p.388 & 393.
302 Knight's Cross, by David Fraser, Harper Collins, NY, NY. 1955. p. 532.
303 Author's Note Dr. Goerdeler, the Mayor of Leipzig was the civilian head of the plot to kill Hitler, and his intent was to be the next Chancellor of Germany. His fellow plotters were Dr. Strolin, Mayor of Stuttgart, Gen. Speidel and Gen. von Kluge. Dr. Strolin was a personal friend of Rommel, having both served together in WWI, survived the Gestapo's investigations. Speidel escaped to the west, von Kluge committed suicide, Goerdeler was executed. Rommel, The Trail of the Fox, by David Irving, Wordsworth Editions, Hertfordshire, England. 1999. pp. 347, 373, 391. Knight's Cross, by David Fraser, Harper Collins, NY, NY. 1955. pp. 511, 527, 531. Rommel, The Desert Fox, by Desmond Young, Quill-William Morrow & Co., NY, NY. 1978. p. 195.

to be President of the Reich when Hitler was gone. My name was on the list. They say that von Stulpnagel, Speidel and von Hofacker have implicated me, as well. The Fuhrer has given me a choice of taking poison or present myself before the People's Court. Either way the results will be the same. I have chosen to take the poison." Frau Rommel begged him to choose the Court. Rommel said, "No, if I chose the Court, we will be dragged through the system. In the end, I will be hanged, and what will happen to you and Manfred? No, I will take the poison, they promised me no harm will come to you, you will receive a Field Marshal's pension, there will be a state funeral, and I can be buried at home."[304] Then Rommel dressed in his Afrika Korps tunic with the Pour le Merite around his neck, bids farewell to his family and staff. As he approaches the car, General Burgdorf acknowledges him with a salute along with the words, "Herr Field Marshal."[305] The car drives off, twenty-five minutes later, the phone rings at Rommel's home. His Aide, Aldinger, answers. It is Major Ehrenberger, who had accompanied the two General's. He says something terrible has happened. The Field Marshall has had a brain hemorrhage. "Rommel is dead."[306]

304 Rommel, The Desert Fox, by Desmond Young, Quill-William Morrow & Co., NY, NY. 1978. pp. 208-210.
305 Rommel, The Trail of the Fox, by David Irving, Wordsworth Editions, Hertfordshire, England. 1999. p. 402 & p. 404
306 Rommel, The Desert Fox, by Desmond Young, Quill-William Morrow & Co., NY, NY. 1978. Pp.210-211.

Desmond Young, author of *Rommel , The Desert Fox*, stated, "Hitler wanted to kill Rommel, it would seem, not so much for being a traitor as for being right when he himself, Keitel, and Jodl were wrong over Africa and again over Normandy. For that he had come to hate Rommel and hatred in this case had only one form of expression."

David Fraser, author of *Knight's Cross*, stated, that Frau Lucy Rommel's last statement concerning her husband's fate was, "Thus ended the life of a man who had devoted his entire self throughout his time to the service of his country."

Immediately after Rommel's forced suicide, Frau Rommel recognized a look of deep contempt on his death face.

Transcription Evolution Astrology
- Astrology by Kim Marie

Erwin Rommel . . . what I'm going to do is just read what I see in the chart. I have no idea who this gentleman is.

This gentleman has the sun conjunct the South Node and you will find this in charts of people who have a very driven personality. And, in his case, because it was in the 10th House of Career, he was very driven to achieve his career. He's a Scorpio, so he's very emotionally driven to do the best that he can do in whatever his given occupation is. He also has Mercury conjunct the South Node and Mercury's in Sagittarius. It's barely in the 10th House of Career. He was always wanting to be heard. He believed that he had a lot of strong message to bring through for people. Venus has got a wide conjunction to that South Node, closer to conjuncting Mercury. There was a part of himself that came through with his own ideas in context to his environment. He had a bit of a different opinion and sometimes that would have been accepted and sometimes not. This is a gentleman who questioned what his belief system was.

The mid-heaven in Erwin's chart is Scorpio. And, this can be the driven scientist, the driven military officer, the driven healer. Scorpio energy on the top of the chart on the mid-heaven is always a desire to really get beneath the surface and go somewhere with it. The t-square in the chart has on one end of the t-square Mercury, Venus and Sagittarius, which means we're either great liars or we're a voice of truth. It opposes Neptune/Pluto conjunct and Gemini in the 5th House. What this meant is, this was an individual who was really trying to break free from any conditioning beliefs that were thrown upon him. This is all oppose of Gemini -Sagittarius, which means that there were times when he would really want to speak his truth and there were times when he would realize that if he did, he could easily lose his life.

Now, from the opposition, we then have the planet Jupiter coming at the bottom and in astrology makes what we call a t-square. Jupiter comes in and relieves the tension created by the opposition. This is a chart of someone who was caught up in this big conflict by really wanting to bust out and speak his truth; someone who asked questions throughout his life, someone who wanted to speak up as a voice of truth.

Again, whether or not he, he did that, I don't know. I don't know anything about this person only what I see in the chart.

With the Neptune-Pluto conjunction in his chart, this gentleman was so highly intuitive. He could walk into a room and just by intuition, tell who was standing in his truth and who was telling a lie. This is an

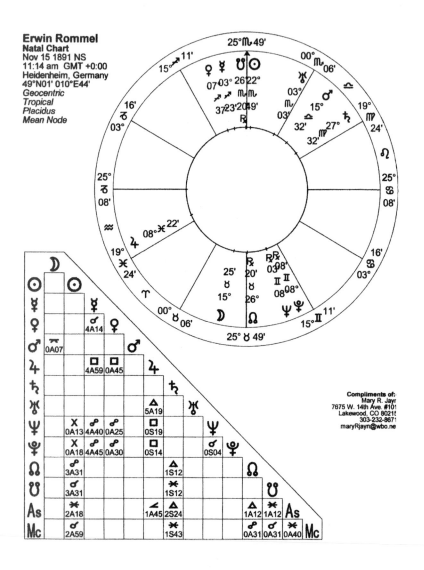

Erwin Rommel
Natal Chart
Nov 15 1891 NS
11:14 am GMT +0:00
Heidenheim, Germany
49°N01' 010°E44'
Geocentric
Tropical
Placidus
Mean Node

Compliments of:
Mary R. Jayr
7675 W. 14th Ave. #101
Lakewood, CO 80215
303-232-8671
maryRjayn@wbo.ne

extremely intuitive chart, but this is not a man who would necessarily show it. He had a Capricorn rising, so his instinctual response to everything in his environment was one of protection, protecting himself and those around him. He may sense things, but that did not mean that he would necessarily speak up and say it. Looking at Jupiter, which represents life, being in the 2nd House, also being in Pisces, positioned with the t-square caused the gentleman who if trying to speak up for the truth and could not do it, would either die speaking up for the truth or he could choose to leave. Leave being a form of suicide.*

* Author's Note: This is the real reason for Rommel's suicide. It is in his birth chart. He knew even before he was born that this was the method he would leave earth's plane. He came into earth's plane with a mission to accomplish. This he did then he returned to the spirit realm.

APPENDIX
LIST OF ILLUSTRATIONS

MAPS

Drawn by A.C. Ross, computer enhanced by Spizzirri Press, Rapid City, SD.

Source: World War I, Gulf of Trieste, Adriatic Sea.
          Fraser, David, Knight's Cross, p. 64.

          World War II, Path of the Ghost Division.
          Liddell-Hart, B.H. Editor, The RommellPapers,
          p. 5.

          North Africa, Afrika Korps Campaign.
          Ellis, Chris, 21st Panzer Division, pp. 20-62.

          Plan Orient
          Fraser, David, Knight's Cross, p. 222.

          The Battle of Kasserine Pass
          Liddell-Hart, B.H. Editor, The Rommell
          Papers, p. 5.

          German Defense Positions on D-Day
          Landing.
          Liddell-Hart, B.H., Editor. The Rommel
          Papers, p. 472.

BIBLIOGRAPHY

Alemanni. Chambers Encyclopedia. Collier Publisher, 1890.

Axis. The New American Webster Handy College Dictionary. NY, NY, Penguin Books, 1995.

Dijkstra, Henk, Editor. History of the Ancient & Medival World. Terrytown, NY, Marshall Cavendish Corporation, 1996.

Ellis, Chris, 21st Panzer Division, Rommel's Afrika Korps Spearhead. Hersham, Surrey, UK. Ian Allan Publishing, 2001.

Fraser, David. Knight's Cross New York: Harper Perennial, 1995.

Hart, B.H. Liddell. The Rommel Papers New York: Da Capo Press, 1953.

Irving, David. Rommel: The Trail of the Fox Hertfordshire: Wordsworth Editions, 1999.

Skelton, R.A., Marston, Thomas E. and Painter, George D. The Finland Map and the Tarter Relation.

New Haven, Conn., New Haven and
London/Yale University Press, 1995.

The Thule Society,
www.crystalinks.com/thule.htm/ from <u>The
Unknown Hitler</u>, by Wulf Schwartzwaller,
Berkeley Books, 1990.

Young, Desmond. <u>Rommel, the Desert Fox</u>
New York: Quill William Morrow

Additional material that was previewed for this book,
but was not specifically used in the composition of this
book.

ADDITIONAL BIBLIOGRAPHY

Blumenson, Martin. <u>Kasserine Pass</u>.
NY, NY, Cooper Square Press, 2000.

Pool, James & Suzanne. <u>Who Financed Hitler</u>.
NY, NY, Dial Press, 1979.

VIDEO

Duel in the Desert.
The History Channel, A&E Television Network,
NY, NY, New Video Group, 1999.

Operation Barbarossa.
Batty, Peter, Producer, New Star Video, 1988.

Rommel, The Last Knight.
Reda, Lou, Producer, A&E Television/Network,
NY, NY, New Video Group, 1997.

PHOTOS

Permission to use the photograph of Field Marshal
Rommel was given by his son Manfred Rommel,
Stuttgart, Germany

Permission to use the photograph of the 88mm Flak
Gun was given by Andreas Altenburger, Stuttgart
www.lexikonderwehrmacht.de

Permission to use the photograph of the Panzer III was
given by Hermann Vogt, Aschaffenburg, Germany

SECTION III
COMPARISON
CRAZY HORSE and ROMMEL

1. Both were born into middle class family. Crazy Horse p.2 and Rommel p.79

2. Both were born into a society that held the warrior in high esteem. Crazy Horse p.2 and Rommel p. 79

3. Both came from historic tribal backgrounds. Crazy Horse p.2 and Rommel p.78

4. Both had origin stories of their people, which were the same. Crazy Horse p.iii and Rommel p.78 see footnote #3

5. Both had childhood nicknames. Crazy Horse p.2 and Rommell p.79

6. Both were of medium height and build. Crazy Horse p.12 and Rommel p.83

7. Both spoke a dialect of their language. Crazy Horse p.2 and Rommel p.79

8. Both did not speak English. Crazy Horse p.2 and Rommel p.79

9. Both had only one true love in their life. Crazy Horse p.11 and Rommel p.81

10. Both had only one child. Crazy Horse p.24 and Rommel p.91

11. Both could go for long periods without food or water. Crazy Horse p.7 and Rommel p.85

12. Both were great horsemen. Crazy Horse p.12 and Rommel p.91

13. Both had a dislike for politics. Crazy Horse p.28 and Rommel p.93

14. Both would walk alone, when pondering an important question. Crazy Horse p.35 and Rommel p.128

15. Both used their 6th sense in battle. Crazy Horse p.16-19 and Rommel p.107

16. Both were courageous warriors. Crazy Horse p.16-19 and Rommel p.87-89

17. Both led from the forward position when in battle. Crazy Horse p.30 and Rommel p.98

18. Both used decoy and deception as military tactics. Crazy Horse p.18 and Rommel p.105

19. Both were wounded in the "same" leg in battle. Crazy Horse p.12 and Rommel p.83

20. Both fought against superior forces. Crazy Horse p. 33 and Rommel p.112-114

21. Both fought the U.S. Army. Crazy Horse p.16 and Rommel p.135

22. Both had victories against the U.S. Army. Crazy Horse p.19 and Rommel p.135

23. Both won battles, but lost the war. Crazy Horse p.35 and Rommel p.148

24. Both used captured enemy arms against the enemy. Crazy Horse p.19 and Rommel p.110

25. Both were great military leaders. Crazy Horse p.31 and Rommel p.88, p.100

26. Both fought withdrawal actions, but were not subdued. Crazy Horse p.33-34 and Rommel p.128-133

27. Both cared for their people dearly. Crazy Horse p.35 and Rommel p.128, p.152

28. Both were heros among their own people. Crazy Horse p.35 and Rommel p.103

29. Both were never defeated in battle. Crazy Horse p.36 and Rommel p.149

30. Both were never captured by the enemy. Crazy Horse p.37 and Rommel p.151

31. Both were despised by members of their own people. Crazy Horse p.36 and Rommel p.103

32. Both were betrayed by members of their own people. Crazy Horse p.36 and Rommel p.151

33. Both had their command taken away from them. Crazy Horse p.23 and Rommel p.134

34. Both knew they were going to die before they did. Crazy Horse p.38 and Rommel p151

35. Both committed suicide. Crazy Horse p.38 (Crazy Horse went to Ft. Robinson knowing he would be killed, this is a form of suicide.) and Rommel p.151

36. Both were honored by their enemies. Crazy Horse p.36 and Rommel p.122, p.127 (Rommel was well respected by the British for his treatment of prisoners)

37. Both honored the enemy by having respect for their lives. Crazy Horse P.12 and Rommel P.121

SECTION IV
ONE THOUSAND YEARS OF PEACE

In Oglala Religion by William K. Powers, Dakota/Lakota language structures identified that separate lexical categories are not employed to differentiate between time and space. Time and space are inseparable. All temporal statements in the Dakota/Lakota languages are simultaneously spatial. Example: A simple sentence in Lakota is, "Letan Pine Ridge towhan hwo." The Literal English interpretation is "When is Pine Ridge from here?" But in the English language, the same sentence is usually stated, "How far is it to Pine Ridge?" indicating left-brain dominance. Thus, in the Lakota language, the spatial or right brain orientation is dominant.

Marilyn Ferguson said in the Aquarian Conspiracy that European languages trap us in a model of understanding that is piecemeal. They pay no attention to relationships by their subject/predicate structure, thus molding our thought patterns by making us think in terms of simple cause and effect. She further stated that, "...for this reason it is hard for us to talk about or even think about quantum physics, the fourth dimension, or any other notion without clear-cut beginning and ending, up and down, then and now."

Modern science has discovered that there is something in the cosmos that is not in accord with the something in the cosmos that is not in accord with the concepts that modern man has formed. Charlton Laird's book Language in America recorded that linguist Benjamin Whorf suggested that the Hopi language, if it will not help scientists find a new language they need, may at least help them see what is wrong with the old one. My interpretation of this is that Native American languages allow more right-brain expression, whereas European languages encourage almost solely left-brain expression.

A Hopi prophecy told about two brothers - one white and a one red. The white brother went to the other side of the planet and will return one day. When he comes back, the two brothers will sit down together and learn each other's language. After that, their two lifeways will entwine and become one.

When I heard this prophecy, what first occurred to me was the information about the left and right hemispheres of the brain. To me, the white brother would be left-brain dominant, and the red brother would be right-brain dominant because of their differing language structures. After we learn each other's ways, we will become whole-brain thinkers. [1]

Hopi spiritual leader Dan Katchongva stated that if the races become separated from each other and no longer know their original teachings, the Creator would cause three world-shaking events to remind them that

[1] Ross, Mitakuye Oyasin, "We are all Related", pg.56-57.

Prophecy Rock Petroglyph

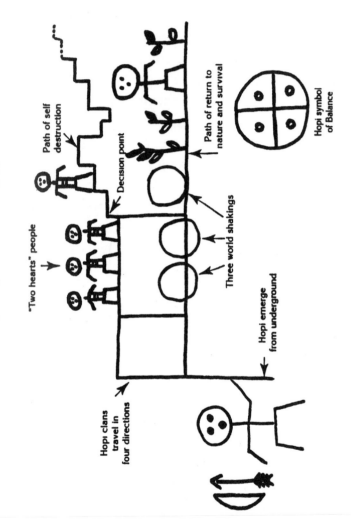

"we are all related." The story connected to the Hopi prophecy rock tells of a time when the Hopi emerged from the underground. The leading clans went in the four directions, then turned right, thus forming a Swastika symbol. The leading clans were: Fire, Spider, Eagle, Kachina, Bear, Badger, Flute, Snake.

The second group of clans which came out of the underground also went out in the four directions, then turned left, thus forming a Swastika in the opposite direction. These clans were named: Butterfly, Bluebird, Crow, Crane, Corn, Pumpkin, Sun, Lizard.

As the Hopi spread knowledge and information around the world, people would gradually become "two hearts," people who think with their head rather than their hearts.

Is it coincidence or synchronicity that the people of Earth today are left brain dominant? Left-brain dominant is to use rational thinking only versus the right-brain function of intuitive thinking. The Hopi prophecy rock goes on to show how man will reach a point where he can make a decision to either continue on the road of thinking with his head only or return to the road of thinking with his heart. If we continue thinking with our head only (rational), we will eventually destroy ourselves. If we take the road of thinking with our heart (intuition) we will eventually return to respect for nature and our survival. On the prophecy rock are also three circles, which represent the three world-shaking events (purifications) which are to remind us of our relativeness. Each of the shakings would be accompanied by a symbol. The symbol for the first shaking would be a "bug on a black ribbon being tossed into the sky." This was interpreted as an airplane. The time when airplanes were first used in war was World War I. So this was the first world shaking. The symbol for the second shaking would be when man used the Hopi migration symbol (Swastika) for war. This was in World War II. So this was the second world shaking. The symbol for the third world shaking would be the color red (a red covering of cloak). Will there be a World War III? The Hopi prophecy rock predicts the third shaking to be a time of total destruction or total rebirth. It is interesting to note that Nostradamus predicted World War III to start January 1991 and to last for ten years. The Hopi say that signs of the third shaking would be when:

1. Trees will die (unknown disease kills palm trees in Florida).
2. Man will build a house in the sky (sky lab?).
3. Cold places become hot, and hot places become cold (global warming?)
4. Land will sink, and land will rise (volcanoes in Iceland cause new land?).
5. There is an appearance of the Blue Star Kachina (Hale-Bopp?).

The Hopi say man needs to return to the original teachings if we want to survive the third world shaking. [2]

The Hopi say man needs to return to the original teachings if we want to survive the third world shaking. [2]

Chief Seattle of the Suquamish, when asked by the government to sell the tribe's land stated the following. These are excerpts from his speech, which was titled, "How can one sell the air?"

We will consider your offer to buy our land.

Do not send men asking us to decide more quickly. We will decide in our time.

Should we accept, I here and now make this condition: we will never be denied the right to walk softly over the grave of our fathers, mothers, and friends, nor may the white man desecrate these graves.

The graves must always be open to the sunlight and the falling rain.

Then the water will fall gently upon the green sprouts and sleep slowly down to moisten the parched lips of our ancestors and quench their thirst.

Every part of this earth is sacred to my people.

Every hillside, every valley, every clearing and wood, is holy in the memory and experience of my people.

Even those unspeaking stones along the shore are loud with the events and memories in the life of my people.

---

[2] *Ibid, pg.226-228.*

The ground beneath your feet responds more lovingly to our steps than yours, because it is the ashes of our grand-fathers.

Our bare feet know the kindred touch.

The earth is rich with the lives of our kin.

Men come and go, like the waves of the sea.

A tear, a prayer to the Great Spirit, a dirge (lament), and they are gone from our longing eyes forever.

Even the white man, whose God walked and talked with him as friend to friend, cannot be exempt from the common destiny.

We may be brothers after all. We shall see. [3]

Black Elk said the 7th holy rite of the Oglala was the "throwing of the ball ceremony." This game represented man's life. He said the playing field stood for the universe; the center of the playing field represented Wakan Tanka or God. The ball also represented Wakan Tanka. The buffalo had no hands and couldn't catch the ball, a representation of ignorance or walking the Black Road.

In The Sacred Pipe Joseph Epes Brown recorded Black Elk's words:

"I, Black Elk, should now explain to you several things that you may not understand about his holy rite. First, it is a little girl, and not an older person, who stands at the center and who throws the ball. This is as

---

[3] *Ibid, pg.228-231.*

it should be, for just as Wakan Tanka is eternally youthful and pure, so is this little one who has just come from Wakan Tanka, pure and without any darkness. Just as the ball is thrown from the center to the four quarters, so Wakan Tanka is at every direction and is everywhere in the world; and as the ball descends upon the people, so does His power, which is only received by a very few people, especially in these last days.

"You have seen that the four-legged buffalo people were not able to play this game with the ball, and so they gave it to the two legged. This is very true because, as I have said before, of all the created things or beings of the universe, it is the two-legged men alone who, if they purify and humiliate themselves, may become one with - or may know - Wakan Tanka.

"At his sad time today among our people we are scrambling for the ball, and some are not even trying to catch it, which makes me cry when I think of it. But soon I know it will be caught, for the end is rapidly approaching, and then it will be returned to the center, and our people will be with it. It is my prayer that this be so, and it is in order to aid in this 'recovery of the ball', that I have wished to make this book." [4]

Just before Black Elk's death in the early 1950s, he prophesied that soon someone would catch the ball (become one with Wakan Tanka). In the process of

[4] *Ibid, pg.104.*

catching it, that person would return it to the center of the playing field (center of the universe). This prophecy reminded me of how Dawson No Horse received his power.

Dawson told me that in 1974, while he was still an Episcopal priest, he was drawn to attend the Sun Dance. While observing it, he saw a person standing in the center by the tree. He asked someone standing next to him, "Who is that standing out there?" The man replied, "I don't see anybody."

Wanting an explanation for this vision, Dawson went to Frank Fools Crow, an Oglala holy man. Frank immediately recognized what was happening and told Dawson to fast on the hill for four days and four nights. Dawson said that the first three days, nothing happened-he was only aware of his hunger, his thirst, and insects eating at him. On the fourth day, a thunderstorm appeared and a bolt of lightning came out of the storm and struck right beside him. The man he had seen in his vision at the Sun Dance stood where the lightning had struck. This man's name was Canupa Gluha Mani (Walks with the Pipe).

After Dawson came down from the hill, Fools Crow started teaching him yuwipi songs and how to conduct the ceremony because he knew that Dawson was suppose to become a yuwipi man (a holy man). Canupa Gluha Mani was Dawson's main spirit helper in the yuwipi ceremony.

For seven years Dawson held ceremonies in which hundreds of people were healed. He carried the ball or walked with God for seven years. Then he told his family, "They're calling me on the other side. It's time for me to go." His family said, "Don't talk like that."

"I know that a lot of these things I have done you have a hard time believing," he replied, "but I tell you now that it's time for me to go." And he planned his own funeral. He said all people were welcome to attend, no matter what religion, no matter what race. On January 28, 1982, the body of Dawson Has No Horse died. I believe his spirit returned to the center of the universe.[5]

Black Elk's explanation of the seventh rite and the information coming from the collective unconscious of Edgar Cayce concerning reincarnation, were almost the same. Cayce said that a person is reincarnated again and again until he becomes whole. Each incarnation is an opportunity for the individual to grow and expand. Cayce stated that when one has fulfilled his karmic debts (sins committed in this life and previous lives), then that individual becomes one with God and his will conforms with the will of the Creator, his earthly cycles are finished, and his soul may return to the center of the universe. Is this what happened to Dawson? Did he become one with

5Ibid, pg.105

God? Is Dawson the person who fulfilled Black Elk's prophecy?[6]

In Dakota spirituality, the earth was considered feminine and the people called her Mother Earth. The Dakota hero archetype was also considered feminine and is known as the White Buffalo Calf Maiden. Almost all tribes have a female as their Hero Archetype. The Hopi have Corn Mother, the Navajo have Changing Women, the Taos have Deer Mother, and the Iroquois have the Three Sisters. Cherokee have Corn Women and Apache have White Painted Mother. In The Portable Jung by Joseph Campbell, he states that in the early Christian church, the Trinity was symbolized by a dove named Sophia, which was a feminine entity!

How did modern man become so out of balance in the way he views the world? Was it when he invented a written language? Or was it when he invented time references (calendar/clock)? Or was it when he invented money (which has lead to economic theories)? All of these inventions utilize left brain modes of thought. Consequently, we live in a left brain dominant world (masculine oriented).

According to Rayna Green, author of Women in American Indian Society, information about American Indian women was first documented by the European white male chauvinist, who possessed religious bigotry. Therefore, a clear picture of early American Indian

6 *Ibid, pg.106*

women did not emerge. The truth is that upon the arrival of the European, native women enjoyed suffrage, sexual liberation, social status of matriarchy, and economic independence (since they did the work, they owned the produce/products). At the completion of Dakota ceremonies, we say Mitakuye Oyasin, which in its spiritual context means everything is related. Traditionally, all planting societies were matriarchal and all hunting societies were patriarchal. After the Lakota acquired the horse, their culture slowly changed form that of a planting society to that of the hunter. But the respect for the feminine has remained among our people. According to the psychic prophet Edgar Cayce, "Entropy of the masculine and feminine energy would begin in 1933. At that time, souls of an androgynous nature would enter the new born bodies here on earth." This may be the reason for male bodies acting more feminine and female bodies acting masculine nowadays. This is good because it provides a balance of the Anima (female) within the male, and the Animus (male) within the female. Edgar Cayce states that the influx of the androgynous souls would continue for 100 years. These androgynous bodies will be the next root race to enter earth's plane, and they will create the thousand years of peace of which the Bible speaks.[7]

In the old days, a person would go on a vision quest to find out what he was good at or what his purpose in life might be. Today, we use astrology. Astrology

7 Ross, *Keeper of the Female Medicine Bundle*, pg.229-231.

is a picture of the heavens the moment you are born. From this picture or Star Map, a skilled astrologer can determine a person's inclinations for his life. As we move into the next century, I feel that astrology is a valuable tool that could be used in education. In the old days, astrology was considered a joke and teaching was by reward and punishment.

Nowadays, there is a change happening. This shift, which is called "Entropy" in psychological terms, will continue until completed. It is a natural evolutionary cycle. So it is best that we recognize this, accept it, and assist it until balance has been achieved.[8]

Ho Hecetu Yelo
"That's the way it is"

8 Ibid, pg.237-238

EPILOGUE

The spirits of Crazy Horse and Rommel entered earth's plane knowing they were to sacrifice themselves for their people. They also knew they would be on the losing side of a war. In defeat, Crazy Horse and Rommel provided a hero for their vanquished people. The psychological damaged caused by a loss in war has a drastic effect on one's psychic. With out the hero the vanquished people could succumb to a psychosis resulting in death. An example is when the American Indian was forced on to reservations many Indians mysteriously died, cause of death was listed by the U.S. Government as unknown. But we Indians knew it was from the heart ache of being crushed with no avenue to seek help. The Teton Sioux did not have this historical trauma as bad as other tribes because we had the hero image of Crazy Horse to assist us during these early days of traumatic reservation life.

When I was growing up in South Dakota, there was a tremendous amount of animosity between the white man and the Indian. This has slowly changed. Fifty years ago, Crazy Horse and Rommel were despised, but there is a positive side to their story. Psychic, Gordon M. Scallion, stated that the children born today have a greater amount of instinct / intuition. Thus enabling them to be more intelligent. In observing my grandchildren, I have noticed that they learn tasks sooner than I did when I was a child. Crazy Horse and Rommel were fore runners in having instinctive qualities. When used correctly, instinct could be a great benefit to mankind. Crazy Horse and Rommel are two examples that people with a high level of instinct do exist and this high level of instinctive ability is achievable by everyone.

We have entered into a new millennium and according to those who study the heavens, we are now being influenced by the energy of peace, unity and brotherhood. It has been predicted that there will be less fighting and killings. A few months ago, I saw a program on television where the U.S. Marines went on a rescue mission in Somalia using rubber bullets. Crazy Horse and Rommel were forerunners of this concept as well. They believed it was more honorable to touch the enemy rather than kill him. (see pg. 165, #37) World peace got a boost when the attack on the World Trade Center occurred. The attack, no matter how unconscionable an act it was, has a positive side. As a result of the attack, more people are taking a second look at the ethnic background of their neighbor. People are taking extra time trying to get along with one another.

As people educate themselves through books and culture classes, respect for one another can only get better and we owe all the thanks to the influences from heaven.

Mitakuye Oyasin
"We are all related"

Post Script

The experience of reservation life continues to effect
Indian people up to the present day. Case in point: When
attending Bureau of Indian Affairs Schools. Besides not
being able to speak our own language or study our own
history. When we enrolled in school at the beginning of
each year the U.S. Government School officials required
all children to soak their hair in DDT pesticide solution,
usually for several hours. I guess they thought we
Indians were all lousy. The after effect of this soaking is
that many of these children who are now adults, have
acquired Parkinson's Disease. Is there a connection?
Current research states that there is a connection between
pesticides and Parkinson's Disease.

The reservation in South Dakota is the home to the
descendents of Crazy Horse's people and is the poorest
area in the entire United States according to the latest U.S.
census report. They have the highest unemployment rate
and the lowest average life expectancy. Alcohol and drug
abuse is rampant on the reservation. There was no
"Marshall Plan" to help the American Indian after the
Indian wars. We need help, please do not send used
clothes or holiday gifts. We need jobs. We want to earn
our own way. If have any ideas on how to help. Please
contact us at:

Wico'ni Wa ste' "Beautiful Life"
P.O. Box 480005
Denver, CO 80248 USA

We are a non-profit organization under US code 501(c)3
established to help the American Indian in:
1.   Educational Scholarships
2.   Educational Materials and Supplies
3.   Tourism on American Indian reservations
4.   Assistance to American Indian Parkinsons Patients

* All donations are tax-deductible

RECOMMENDED BOOKS TO READ

Encyclopedia of American Indian Contributions to the World: 15,000 Years of Inventions and Innovations by Emory Dean Keoke and Kay Marie Proterfield, Published by Facts on Fire, Inc., New York, NY, ISBN 0816040524

Indian Givers: How the Indians of the Americas Transformed the World by Jack Weatherford, Published by Fawcett Columbine, New York, NY, ISBN 0449904962

Mitakuye Oyasin "We are all Related": America Before Columbus, Based on the Oral History of 33 Tribes by A.C. Ross - (Ehanamani), Published by Wiconi Waste' (Beautiful Life), Denver, CO, ISBN 096219770X

Keeper of the Female Medicine Bundle (The Role of Indian Women in Traditional American Indian Society) by A.C. Ross - (Ehanamani), Published by Wiconi Waste' (Beautiful Life), Denver, CO, ISBN 09621977-77

Lies My Teacher Told Me: Everything Your American History Textbook Got Wrong by James W. Loewen, A Touchstone Book Published by Simon and Schuster, Inc., New York, NY, ISBN 0684818868   (This book tells the true version of the colonist contact with the American Indian.)

MITAKUYE OYASIN

"We are all related"

The history and culture of America before Columbus, based on American Indian oral history. Twenty-six years of research have gone into this book. It is the doctorate dissertation of Lakota Sioux author, Ehanamani "walks among."

The book **MITAKUYE OYASIN** by Ehanamani A. C. Ross compares the legends and cultures of the American Indian with the world's major philosophies and religions.

Topics include:

- Esoteric teachings of the American Indian
- Brain hemisphercy and cultural attitudes
- Spiritual healing
- Black Elk's prophecy
- Strategies for global harmony
- American Indian philosophy
- Origins of the American Indian

ISBN 0-9621977-0X $12.00

MITAKUYE OYASIN
"We are all related"
REVISED EDITION

Dr. A.C. Ross
(Ehanamani)

OVER 60,000 COPIES SOLD

Winner of the 1992 "top 50" Recognition Award at the Frankfurt International Bookfair, **MITAKUYE OYASIN** is being used in over 50 universities and 300 high schools in the areas of: psychology, comparative religions, native American studies, philosophy, counseling and guidance.

In its twelfth printing, the book is a best seller in Europe with translations in French, Russian, German, Japanese and Italian.

A teacher's guide is also available.

The Dakota/Lakota author of *Mitakuye Oyasin* shares a

SUN DANCE EXPERIENCE

This experience led him to discover how American Indian poverty
IS PERPETUATED BY THE FEDERAL RESERVE SYSTEM!

Follow the Ehanamani family from 1863 when it was forced onto the reservation and learn about reservation life from 1940 to the present.

You'll learn:

- The *real reason* behind the slogan "Indian Giver."
- About the Chief Big Foot Ride Prophecy.
- About the Serpent Vision.
- What the term *walk-in* means.
- Where the Bible condemns the charging of interest on monetary loans.
- How encounters of the fourth kind are guiding us into the Future.

ISBN 0-9621977-2-6 $12.00

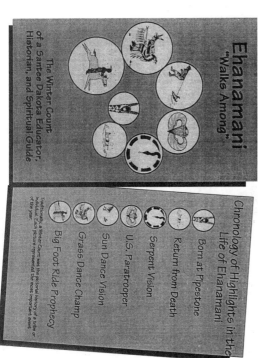

Ehanamani
"Walks Among"

The Winter Count
of a Santee Dakota Educator,
Historian, and Spiritual Guide

Chronology of Highlights in the
Life of Ehanamani

- Born at Pipestone
- Return from Death
- Serpent Vision
- U.S. Paratrooper
- Sun Dance Vision
- Grass Dance Champ
- Big Foot Ride Prophecy

Traditionally, a Winter Count was the pictorial history of a tribe or individual. Each picture represented the most important event of the year.

AMERICAN INDIAN PROPHECIES I

(Ojibwa, Hopi, Paiute, Sioux, Maya, Navajo, and Aztec)

Compared with predictions by:

NOSTRADAMUS
EDGAR CAYCE
RUTH MONTGOMERY
GORDON-MICHAEL SCALLION

Produced by Wicóni Wasté
Narrated by Dr. A.C. Ross
Author of <u>Mitakuye Oyasin</u>
"We are all related"

DISCOVER:

⊳ How to prepare for the coming earth changes
⊳ How the Black Hills can be returned
⊳ When spiritual unity will occur
⊳ What to invest money in for the future
⊳ What is causing the increase in earthquakes, volcanic eruptions, and unknown diseases

MAIL ORDER

HOME VIDEO

VHS - $19.95 + $3.95(S&H) = $23.90
PAL (European) - $29.95 + $8.95(S&H) = $38.90
(We accept Visa/MC)

SEND TO: Wicóni Wasté " Beautiful Life"
P.O. Box 480005
Denver, CO 80248
303-238-3420

AMERICAN INDIAN PROPHECIES I

Sun Dance Vision

Produced by:
Wicóni Wasté
Running Time 1 hr.

AMERICAN INDIAN PROPHECIES II

An Interview With "Ehanamani"

a.k.a.

Dr. A.C. Ross

Due to popular demand, Dr. Ross discusses the prophecies presented in the video, American Indian Prophecies I

Interviewer: John Belindo

Issues to be Discussed:

Δ Return of the White Buffalo
Δ The Mayan calendar's connection to the "Quickening."
Δ Biblical prophecy comparisons
Δ When will spiritual unity occur
Δ Will Tribal Governments survive
Δ Black Elk's Vision of the Flowering Tree
Δ Who is guiding us into the next century

HOME VIDEO

VHS - $19.95 + $3.95(S&H) = $23.90
PAL (European) - $29.95 + $8.95(S&H) = $38.90

(We accept Visa/MC)

SEND TO: Wicóni Wasté " Beautiful Life "
P.O. Box 480005
Denver, CO 80248
303-238-3420

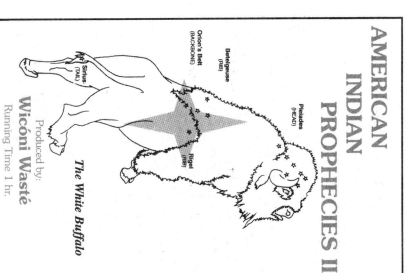

AMERICAN INDIAN PROPHECIES II

Pleiades (HEAD)
Betelgeuse (RIB)
Orion's Belt (BACKBONE)
Sirius (TAIL)
Rigel (RIB)

The White Buffalo

Produced by:
Wicóni Wasté
Running Time 1 hr.

AMERICAN INDIAN PROPHECIES III

An Interview With "Ehanamani"

a.k.a.

Dr. A.C. Ross

Due to popular demand, Dr. Ross discusses additional prophecies

Interviewer: Jeff D. Alley

Issues to be Discussed:

Δ Black Elk's Sacred Hoop of Nations Vision
Δ Will the Sweat Lodge Ceremony Survive?
Δ Dawson No Horse Vision of the Future
Δ Prophecy of the androgynous beings
Δ What is meant by "medium of exchange"
Δ A dream about the American Indian Prophecy videos
Δ Wounded Knee memorial ride prophecy

HOME VIDEO

VHS - $19.95 + $3.95 (S&H) = $23.90
PAL (European) - $29.95 + $8.95 (S&H) = $38.90
(We accept Visa/MC)

MAIL ORDER

SEND TO: **Wicóni Wasté "Beautiful Life"**
P.O. Box 480005
Denver, CO 80248
303-238-3420

AMERICAN INDIAN PROPHECIES III

Wounded Knee Memorial Ride Prophecy

Produced by:
Wicóni Wasté

Running Time 55 min.

HALE – BOPP
COMET OR STAR?

A Presentation by Ehanamani
a.k.a.
Dr. A.C. Ross

A Comparison of information concerning the HALE – BOPP comet.

Topics Presented:

Δ Learn the correlation between the Blue Star and the comet Hale – Bopp.

Δ What do the Hopi / Lakota have in common with the Blue Star.

Δ Discover the connection between the Bible and Hale – Bopp

Δ Is Hale – Bopp a harbinger for destruction or peace?

Δ Why has NASA discontinued publishing information concerning Hale – Bopp?

Δ Is there a correlation between Hale – Bopp and the 12th planet?

Δ Learn how Hale – Bopp is ushering in the second coming.

MAIL ORDER

HOME VIDEO

VHS - $19.95 + $3.95(S&H) = $23.90

PAL (European) - $29.95 + $8.95(S&H) = $38.90

(We accept Visa/MC)

SEND TO: Wicóni Waste "Beautiful Life"
P.O. Box 480005
Denver, CO 80248
303-238-3420

HALE – BOPP: COMET OR STAR?
Wicóni Waste – copyright 1997

ISBN 0-9621977-6-9

AMERICAN INDIAN PROPHECIES IV

HALE – BOPP
PROPHECY STAR?

Produced by:
Wicóni Waste
Running Time 1 hour

KEEPER OF THE FEMALE MEDICINE BUNDLE

A book filled with the wisdom of the Elders

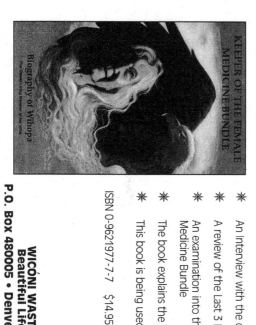

KEEPER OF THE FEMALE
MEDICINE BUNDLE

Biography of Wihopa
The Caretaking Keeper of the Sou

❋ An interview with the oldest living member of her tribe

❋ A review of the Last 3 Keepers of the Female Medicine Bundle

❋ An examination into the life of the Present Keeper of the Female Medicine Bundle

❋ The book explains the future of feminine energy

❋ This book is being used in female studies programs

ISBN 0-9621977-7-7 $14.95

WICÓNI WASTÉ
Beautiful Life
P.O. Box 480005 • Denver, CO 80248

Released in1998

Limited Edition

VIDEO
MAIL ORDER FORM

American Indian Prophecy Videos I, II, III and IV

ORDER FORM

Name _____

Address _____

City _____ State _____ Zip _____

Qty	Title	Price/Video	Total
	VIDEO	$19.95 EA	
	SET (4 VIDEOS)	$59.95 EA	
	POSTAGE (BOOK RATE)		
	VIDEO	$ 3.95 EA	
	1 SET (4 VIDEOS)	$ 5.95	
	Handling ($1.50 per order)		$ 1.50
	TOTAL		

Air Mail: For orders from outside the USA, add $5.00 per video. For orders from outside North America, add $8.00 per video.

Make checks, money orders and purchase orders payable to:
Wicóni Wasté – "Beautiful Life"
PO BOX 480005
DENVER, CO 80248
303-238-3420

CREDIT CARD ORDERS WELCOMED (VISA/MC)

BOOKS

ORDER FORM

Name _____

Address _____

City _____ State _____ Zip _____

Qty	Title	Price	Total
	EHANAMANI	$12.00 EA	
	MITAKUYE OYASIN	$12.00 EA	
	KEEPER - FEMALE BUNDLE	$14.95	
	CRAZY HORSE	$10.95	
		SUBTOTAL	
		Postage (see below)	
	Handling ($1.50 per order)		$1.50
		TOTAL	

Postage (Priority)
1-4 copies $3.95
5 or more copies   .80 per book

Air Mail: For orders outside the U.S., add $5.00 per book. For other international orders, add $8.00 per book.

Make checks, money orders and purchase orders payable to:
   Wicóni Wasté
   P.O. BOX 480005
   DENVER, CO 80248

For wholesale orders, contact:
   New Leaf Distributing
   401 Thornton Road
   Lithia Springs, GA 30122

CREDIT CARD ORDERS WELCOMED

ABOUT THE AUTHOR

Ehanamani (Walks Among) a.k.a A.C. Ross is the chief of the Black Hills Sundance he also has worked for 27 years in the field of education as a teacher, principal, superintendent, college professor and college department chairman. He left formal education 10 years ago to promote his book entitled Mitakuye Oyasin "We are all Related". It won the top book award at Europe's largest book fair in 1992. It is now a best seller in the 16th printing with over 100,000 copies sold.

A.C. Ross' second book Ehanamani "Walks Among" is in the 8th printing. His third book Keeper of the Female Medicine Bundle is in the 6th printing, and Crazy Horse his 4th book is in the 5th printing.

A.C. Ross has lectured on cultural understanding in 44 states in the U.S., 6 Canadian provinces, 10 European countries and most recently, Japan.